THE NEWBERY AND CALDECOTT BOOKS IN THE CLASSROOM

by Claudette Hegel Comfort

Incentive Publications, Inc.
Nashville, Tennessee

Cover designed by Susan Eaddy
Edited by Sherri Y. Lewis

ISBN 0-86530-178-6

Table Of Contents

CALDECOTT

INTRODUCTION

If you've been using library books to teach your students reading, this source is a guide to using the Newbery and Caldecott Medal Winners (voted "the most distinguished contribution to children's literature" for that year) as part of your reading program!

Included in the front matter are discussion and activity ideas to be used with all books referenced.

Each one-page entry contains an overview of the book, discussion topics, and correlated activities. Since the discussion questions are open-ended, students will like the no right/wrong answer approach. The out-of-the-ordinary activities included for each title encourage children to use their imaginations by writing their own folktales, using resources books to find out more about a topic, acting out scenes in the book, and more.

THE NEWBERY AND CALDECOTT BOOKS IN THE CLASSROOM will help you begin or continue an award-winning reading program by providing an easy-to-use format with award-winning books!

1. What does the picture on the cover tell about the book?

2. What does the title tell about the book? What other titles would work?

3. How much about the book does the first page reveal?

4. Describe the main character's and/or other characters' physical traits, personality traits, hobbies, etc.

5. Put yourself in the main character's or another character's place. What would you do differently? Why?

6. How would the book be different if told in another character's perspective?

7. How would the book be different if set in another time (earlier or later)? Place?

8. How could the ending be different?

9. How could the book be improved?

10. Would the book make a good movie or television show? Why or why not?

11. If the book were made into a movie, which actors and actresses would you like to see in the main roles?

12. What did you learn from the book?

13. Did the book deserve to win an award? Why or why not?

14. Why do you think the author wrote the book?

15. What do you like best and least about the book? Why?

ACTIVITIES *All Books*

1. Before you read the book for the first time, read a chapter or a few pages from the middle of the book. Tell or write a summary of what you think happens before and after the passage you read. Read the book; then tell how your ideas were similar and different from the actual version.

2. Make anagrams of the titles, authors, and/or illustrators.

3. Dramatize a scene from the book.

4. Write an ad for a newspaper classified column ("For Sale," "Lost and Found," "Help Wanted," etc.) about the book.

5. Create a crossword, find-a-word, or other pencil puzzle about the book. Make a class book from the results.

6. Make up jokes or riddles about the book.

7. Play charades with titles or phrases from the book.

8. Write a poem or song about the book.

9. Select a panel to debate various instances from the book.

10. Make a picture book version of nonpicture books.

11. Find out more about the author and/or illustrator.

12. Make a report card for each book. Include grades for character, setting, plot, illustrations, etc.

13. Describe a scene from the book as if you are an on-the-spot reporter.

14. Make up a board game or physical game based on the book.

15. Pick a book you think each of the characters would enjoy and dislike, and tell why.

16. Design a poster for the book.

17. Watch a video or listen to a recording of the book and compare it with the written version of the book.

18. Make a Christmas tree ornament based on the book.

19. Create a book jacket, or make a bookmark for the book.

20. Make a list of questions you'd like to ask the author about the book.

21. List the sights, sounds, smells, tastes, and feelings (physical and emotional) mentioned in the book.

22. Think of advertising slogans (from other products or original) that could be used for the book.

23. Design a bulletin board about the book.

24. List several questions whose answers can be found in the book and "test" your friends.

25. Make up a commercial (audio and/or visual) for the book.

26. Make a list of questions you'd like to ask a character.

27. Make a timeline and/or mural of the events in the book.

28. Draw a map of its setting.

29. Write your review of the book.

30. Put on a puppet show of the book.

31. Dress up as one of the characters.

32. Make a mobile of significant articles from the book.

33. Write a journal entry as if you were one of the characters.

34. Make a collage of drawn or cutout pictures that will identify the book.

35. Write a thank-you letter to the author, and/or illustrator, and/or publisher.

36. Pretend to be a character from the book for a specified length of time.

37. Read other books by the same author.

38. Find a review of the book in a magazine or book.

39. Write about or draw a picture with an example of what makes the main character noteworthy.

40. Make flash cards of recognizable names, events, etc., from several books.

THE STORY OF MANKIND

written and illustrated by Hendrik Van Loon
published by Liveright, 1921

ABOUT THE BOOK

The major events of history from the time earth was formed through World War II are explained. This history involves names, places, dates, and why things happened.

FOR DISCUSSION

1. What was your favorite and least favorite time in history? Why?

2. How much of the history did you know before reading the book? What was the biggest surprise you had while reading the book? Why?

3. What events mentioned in the book would you like to know more about? Why?

4. What major events have happened since the book was written?

5. The dedication of the book includes a quotation from *Alice In Wonderland* (" 'What is the use of a book without pictures?' said Alice." What part do the illustrations play in this book?

ACTIVITIES

1. Make a timeline of the events in this book.

2. Read a book from the reading list included at the end of the book. Give a written or oral report on the book.

3. Make up a trivia game of questions and answers from the book.

1923

THE VOYAGES OF DOCTOR DOLITTLE

written and illustrated by Hugh Lofting
published by Lippincott, 1922

ABOUT THE BOOK

Dr. Dolittle and 10-year-old Tommy spend two years traveling around the world. They meet a variety of unusual people and adventures in their travels.

FOR DISCUSSION

1. How do you think Tommy felt about being away from his parents so long? How do you think his parents felt?

2. What is your favorite and least favorite adventure from the book? Why?

3. Would you like to work with Dr. Dolittle? Why or why not?

4. Would you enjoy being able to understand and speak to animals? Why or why not?

5. How would people in your community accept someone like Dr. Dolittle? Why?

ACTIVITIES

1. Use a map to chart the possible route Dr. Dolittle and Tommy took.

2. Research scientific experiments on communication with dolphins and monkeys.

3. Watch a pet for several days. Keep notes of the pet's actions and reactions to various things – when you return home from school, when a stranger comes to the door, dinnertime, telephone ringing, etc.

THE DARK FRIGATE

written by Charles Boardman Hawes
illustrated by Anton Otto Fischer
published by Little Brown, 1923

ABOUT THE BOOK
Philip becomes a boatswain aboard a ship after his father's death. The ship is captured by a gang of pirates who force Philip to join them.

FOR DISCUSSION
1. Would you have reacted the same way as Philip did throughout his adventures? Why or why not?

2. Would you like to go on an adventure similar to Philip's? Why or why not?

3. Would you like to be a captain on a ship? Why or why not?

4. Would you like to be a pirate? Why or why not?

5. The language of the book (using "thy" and "nay," etc.) is unfamiliar. Did that add to or detract from your enjoyment of the book? Why?

ACTIVITIES
1. Find a book on making sailor's knots. Practice tying the knots; then make a sampler of them.

2. Research pirates.

3. Write a short story in the language of *The Dark Frigate* or rewrite a passage from the book in modern-day language.

TALES FROM SILVER LANDS

written by Charles Finger
illustrated by Paul Honore
published by Doubleday, 1924

ABOUT THE BOOK

The nineteen legendary tales about jungle animals, fairies, giants, and earth people were collected firsthand from the South American Indians.

FOR DISCUSSION

1. Which story was your favorite? Least favorite? Why?

2. Have you heard other versions of these stories before? How are they alike and different?

3. How would these tales be different if they were set in the United States? Alike?

4. How would the stories be different if they were set in modern times? Alike?

5. The author collected these tales firsthand from South American Indians. Would you like to travel to another part of the world to collect similar tales? Why or why not?

ACTIVITIES

1. Write your own folktale.

2. Rewrite one of the tales in modern-day language.

3. Use a Spanish/English dictionary to look up the names of the characters. Learn a few Spanish words and phrases.

SHEN OF THE SEA

written by Arthur Bowie Chrisman
illustrated by Else Hasselriis
published by Dutton, 1925

ABOUT THE BOOK
Each of the sixteen Chinese stories is humorous, philosophical, wise, or just plain fun. The stories are especially suitable for reading aloud.

FOR DISCUSSION
1. Which story do you like the best? Why? Which story do you like the least? Why?

2. What would American versions of the stories be like? For example, the story "Chopsticks" would need to be "Silverware."

3. Which character in the book would you most like to have as a friend? Why? Which character in the book would you least like to have as a friend? Why?

4. Do the names of the Chinese characters add to or detract from the stories? Why?

5. How much does the title *Shen of the Sea* tell you about the book? Why do you think there is a subtitle of *Chinese Stories for Children*?

ACTIVITIES
1. Select one of the stories and tell or rewrite it so that a younger child could easily understand it.

2. Find another Chinese folktale to share with the class.

3. Make a silhouette picture similar to the ones in the book.

1927

SMOKY, THE COWHORSE

written and illustrated by Will James
published by Scribner, 1926

ABOUT THE BOOK

From the moment of Smoky's birth on the prairie, he encounters one adventure after another. He learns the beauty and danger of nature, meets a special cowboy, and becomes a rodeo star.

FOR DISCUSSION

1. Which of Smoky's adventures do you like the best and the least? Why?

2. Smoky doesn't meet a human until the second chapter. Do you think a whole book could have been written about Smoky if he'd never met a human? Why or why not?

3. What do you like about horses? Why? Dislike? Why?

4. Would you like to be a horse? Why or why not?

5. Many animal-rights activists say rodeos are exploiting animals. Do you agree? Why or why not?

ACTIVITIES

1. Practice lassoing or rope twirling.

2. Act out a colt standing up for the first time.

3. Write a report on a different breed of horse.

GAY-NECK, THE STORY OF A PIGEON

written by Dhan Mukerji
illustrated by Boris Artzybasheff
published by Dutton, 1927

ABOUT THE BOOK
Gay-Neck's owner trains him well, and the bird becomes his prized carrier pigeon. Gay-Neck becomes a hero in India during World War I.

FOR DISCUSSION
1. The book is written in two parts. The first is Gay-Neck's birth and training. The second is his experiences in war. Which do you like better? Why?

2. What do you think Gay-Neck's brother or sister would have been like if the egg hadn't been broken?

3. Why do you think pigeons were chosen as carriers instead of another bird?

4. Would you like to train homing pigeons? Why or why not?

5. What message would you like to send to a friend by carrier pigeon? To your teacher over summer vacation? To a stranger?

ACTIVITIES
1. Use a map to find the places where Gay-Neck visited.

2. Research homing pigeons. Find out if someone in your area trains them. If so, invite him or her to speak.

3. Watch the actions of a bird(s) and keep notes.

THE TRUMPETER OF KRAKOW

written by Eric P. Kelly
illustrated by Aniela Prusynska
new edition illustrated by Janina Domanska
published by Macmillan, 1928

ABOUT THE BOOK

Mystery and intrigue surround a jewel in fifteenth-century Poland. Fifteen-year-old Joseph finally has an opportunity to send a warning through his trumpet's tune.

FOR DISCUSSION

1. What part does the alchemist play in the story? Could he have helped as much if he had another profession? Why or why not?

2. What would the story be like if set in modern-day United States?

3. What would be other good hiding places for the crystal?

4. Was Joseph brave or foolhardy to play the complete song? Why?

5. What could have happened if Elzbietka hadn't heard the complete tune?

ACTIVITIES

1. Play the music from the book as a broken-off tune and complete.

2. Pretend you're Joseph. Write a diary entry after you'd played the complete song.

3. Make a collage of items mentioned in the book (pumpkin, trumpet, tower, etc.).

HITTY: HER FIRST HUNDRED YEARS

written by Rachel Field
illustrated by Dorothy P. Lathrop
published by Macmillan, 1929

ABOUT THE BOOK

Hitty is a wooden doll made from mountain ash. She meets many people, famous and nonfamous; travels the world; and has many unusual adventures in her first hundred years.

FOR DISCUSSION

1. Which event in Hitty's life is most and least believable? Why?

2. Would the book have been better, worse, or the same if Hitty had been in the shape of an animal instead of a doll? Why?

3. What do you think will happen to Hitty in her second hundred years? Third hundred years?

4. Hitty sells for $51 at the end of the book. The book was published in 1929. What do you think the doll would sell for today?

5. Would you like to own Hitty? Why or why not? If yes, how much would you be willing to pay for her? (Note: The author and illustrator bought "Hitty" from an antique dealer. The doll was present at the ceremony awarding the Newbery Medal to the book she inspired.)

ACTIVITIES

1. Trace the route of Hitty's adventures on a map.

2. Make a timeline of Hitty's experiences.

3. Write about the life of one of your possessions.

1931

THE CAT WHO WENT TO HEAVEN

written by Elizabeth Coatsworth
illustrated by Lynd Ward
published by Macmillan, 1930

ABOUT THE BOOK

A poor artist includes several animals in a painting of the last days of Buddha. He risks having the painting rejected by including his cat. The painting results in a miracle.

FOR DISCUSSION

1. Was "Good Fortune" a good name for the cat? Why or why not?

2. The artist was selected because the slip of paper with his name was the only one that didn't blow away. What other random methods of making selections are there? (Flipping coins, "Eeny, meeny, miney, moe," etc.) Is that a good way to select someone of importance? Why or why not?

3. Do you think a cat deserves to be in a painting of Buddha? Why or why not?

4. What would have happened to the artist and the housekeeper if the miracle of the painting hadn't taken place?

ACTIVITIES

1. Draw, paint, or make a collage of a picture like the artist was commissioned to draw.

2. Find superstitions about cats – calico cats in particular.

3. Make up a haiku about the book. A haiku is a Japanese poem of three lines and seventeen syllables (five syllables in the first and third lines and seven syllables in the middle line). An example: The cat Good Fortune/brought luck to the poor artist/and his housekeeper.

WATERLESS MOUNTAIN

written by Laura Adams Armer
illustrated by Sidney and Laura Armer
published by Longmans, 1931

ABOUT THE BOOK
Many Navajo legends and facts are included in the story of Younger Brother as he learns about nature and his heritage.

FOR DISCUSSION
1. How would Younger Brother's life be different if the book were set in the current time?

2. Would you like to live next to nature like Younger Brother? Why or why not?

3. Why is the book valuable in learning about Navajo culture?

4. The author spent many years living among the Navajo Indians. Do you think someone who hadn't lived with the Navajo could have written a book that sounds as authentic as Waterless Mountain? Why or why not?

5. How do you think the Navajo customs have changed since 1931, the year the book was published?

ACTIVITIES
1. Draw or paint your own design as if you were planning to make a Navajo rug or blanket.

2. Find information on current Navajo customs and art. Also, examine the art of making turquoise jewelry.

3. Act out the wedding ceremony in chapter nine.

1933

YOUNG FU OF THE UPPER YANGTZE

written by Elizabeth Lewis
illustrated by Kurt Wiese
published by Winston, 1932

ABOUT THE BOOK
Young Fu lives in China during the Revolution. His many adventures include battling fire, flood, and bandits. Young Fu learns that not all people can be trusted, but kindness can be rewarded.

FOR DISCUSSION
1. How would Young Fu's life have been different if his father had still been alive?

2. If Tang was disappointed in your work, would you have tried harder to produce a quality item as Young Fu did, or would you have given up? Why?

3. Young Fu's experiences included fire, flood, bandits, etc. Do you think the book is a typical story of a boy living in China then? Why or why not?

4. What are some of the superstitions mentioned in the book? How do you think those beliefs started?

5. How has life in China changed since the book was published in 1932?

ACTIVITIES
1. Find and read several sayings of Confucius.

2. Learn a few Chinese words and phrases.

3. Print your name vertically in Chinese-style letters.

INVINCIBLE LOUISA

written by Cornelia Meigs
illustrated with photographs
published by Little Brown, 1933

ABOUT THE BOOK
This biography of Louisa May Alcott and her family tells of their struggles to survive. Louisa finally turns to writing to support the family.

FOR DISCUSSION
1. Why do you think the book's title is *Invincible Louisa*?

2. What do you like best and least about Louisa? Why?

3. How would Louisa's life be different if she were born when your grandparents were? Your parents? You?

4. Do you think Louisa would have been a writer if she didn't have to support her family? Why or why not?

5. Can you think of Louisa as being a real person after reading the book? Why or why not? How does using photographs instead of drawings help to make a character more real?

ACTIVITIES
1. Read one of Louisa's books and prepare an oral or written report on it.

2. Make a timeline of Louisa's life.

3. Find famous quotations by Louisa or her father Amos Bronson Alcott.

1935

DOBRY

written by Monica Shannon
illustrated by Atanas Katchamakoff
published by Viking, 1934

ABOUT THE BOOK

Dobry is a young boy living in Bulgaria. His love of art and his artistic talent are supported by his grandfather, but his practical mother thinks Dobry is wasting his time.

FOR DISCUSSION

1. What purpose(s) do Grandfather's stories play in the book?

2. Why do you think Dobry's mother didn't understand his love of art? Why do you think his grandfather did?

3. Why do you think Dobry looked forward to the gypsy bear's arrival?

4. How do you think Dobry felt while he was drawing or sculpting? When he completed a piece?

5. Name some sights, sounds, tastes, smells, and feelings (physical and emotional) from the book.

ACTIVITIES

1. Pretend you're Dobry. Draw or sculpt something and try to completely lose yourself in the project.

2. Make and/or fly a kite.

3. Grind or pound wheat into flour by hand.

CADDIE WOODLAWN

written by Carol Ryrie Brink
illustrated by Kate Seredy
new edition illustrated by Trina Schart Hyman
published by Macmillan, 1935

ABOUT THE BOOK

Caddie is a tomboy living in Wisconsin in the 1860s. She's a practical joker and a daredevil and still cares deeply for the people around her.

FOR DISCUSSION

1. If you were Caddie, would you have tried to be friends with the Indians? Why or why not?

2. What kind of adventures would Caddie have if she had been shy? If she were living today?

3. If you were Caddie, how would you spend the dollar? What do you think today's equivalent of one dollar would be? What would you buy with the equivalent today?

4. How would the ending be different if they went to England?

5. Why do you think the Civil War isn't more prominent in the book?

ACTIVITIES

1. Write to Menomonie, Wisconsin, for information about Caddie's house.

2. Research the massacre in New Ulm.

3. Make a miniature patchwork quilt by hand.

ROLLER SKATES

written by Ruth Sawyer
illustrated by Valenti Angelo
published by Viking, 1936

ABOUT THE BOOK

Lucinda travels on roller skates around the streets of New York. She makes a variety of new friends along the way. These friends affect her in many ways.

FOR DISCUSSION

1. What is Lucinda's most admirable and least admirable character trait? Why?

2. Which of Lucinda's friends would you most like to have for a friend and why? Least like to have for a friend? Why? Would you like to be Lucinda's friend? Why or why not?

3. Reread the last paragraph. Would you like to be ten forever? Why or why not?

4. Are roller skates a good method of transportation? Why or why not?

5. Would Lucinda be as safe being as adventurous today? Why or why not?

ACTIVITIES

1. Keep a diary like Lucinda.

2. Spend a day on roller skates if you know how, or learn to roller skate if you don't.

3. Read one of Shakespeare's plays (or an adaptation of one).

THE WHITE STAG

written and illustrated by Kate Seredy
published by Viking, 1937

ABOUT THE BOOK
The Mighty God Hadur sends the White Stag to lead Atilla the Hun and the Hungarians to new lands.

FOR DISCUSSION
1. Why do you think Hunor and Magyar were represented by eagles?

2. How would you feel about leaving your home to go on a long trek to a new "promised land"?

3. Why do you think a White Stag was chosen to lead them?

4. Would you like to be a leader of people going to a new area? Why or why not?

5. How much of the story do you think is true? Why?

ACTIVITIES
1. Follow the path of the Huns and Magyars on a map, or draw your own map.

2. Research Atilla the Hun.

3. Select a part of the text with dialogue and perform a dramatic reading.

THIMBLE SUMMER

written and illustrated by Elizabeth Enright
published by Rinehart, 1938

ABOUT THE BOOK

Garnet finds a silver thimble which seems to make the summer magic. Entering her pig in competition at the fair, watching a new barn being built, and accepting an orphan into the family are only a few of her adventures.

FOR DISCUSSION

1. What role did the thimble play in the events of the summer?

2. What would you do if you were locked in a library for several hours?

3. What is your favorite and least favorite event at a fair? Why?

4. How has farm living changed since Garnet's day? How is it the same?

5. Would you prefer to live on a farm, in a small town, or in a large city? Why? Where would you least like to live? Why?

ACTIVITIES

1. Plant oats in a large container. Make notes of the growth.

2. Organize a debate of city living versus farm living.

3. Find out how livestock is judged at a fair. If possible, invite a judge to speak. Contact 4-H or county extension offices for information.

DANIEL BOONE

written and illustrated by James Daugherty
published by Viking, 1939

ABOUT THE BOOK

The author followed the route of Daniel Boone to help him prepare to write this biography. The book depicts Daniel's courage and interest in exploring the wilderness around him.

FOR DISCUSSION

1. What do you like best and least about Daniel Boone? Why?

2. Why do you think Daniel and John James Audubon were friends?

3. What did you learn about Daniel Boone that you didn't know before?

4. What would Daniel Boone be like if he were living today (jobs, how famous, etc.)?

5. *Daniel Boone* is one of the few Newbery Medal books to ever go out of print. Why do you think it did?

ACTIVITIES

1. Go on a nature walk.

2. Read other books about Daniel Boone. Compare the facts mentioned in them.

3. Follow Daniel's path on a map or draw your own.

1941

CALL IT COURAGE

written and illustrated by Armstrong Sperry
published by Macmillan, 1940

ABOUT THE BOOK

Mafatu, son of the Great Chief, is often ridiculed for being afraid of the sea. To prove his courage, Mafatu goes off in a small canoe. A storm strands him on a desert island where he must face many dangers.

FOR DISCUSSION

1. Why do you think Mafatu was afraid of the sea?

2. Why was a knife so important to Mafatu?

3. Why do you think Mafatu made the boar's tooth necklace? What did it represent?

4. Do you think Mafatu lived after he collapsed into his father's arms? Why or why not?

5. Would you like to spend time alone on an island? Why or why not? How long minimum? Maximum?

ACTIVITIES

1. Make a list of the foreign words and meanings mentioned in the book.

2. Select a different plant or animal on the island and give an oral or written report on it.

3. Write "recipes" of the unusual foods Mafatu made and try them. (Steamed bananas is one example.)

THE MATCHLOCK GUN

written by Walter D. Edmonds
illustrated by Paul Lantz
published by Dodd Mead, 1941

ABOUT THE BOOK

A boy in Colonial New York is fascinated by an old gun that hangs on the wall. He later fires the gun to save his mother and baby sister from Indians.

FOR DISCUSSION

1. Why do you think Edward was so fascinated by the gun?

2. Why do you think Gertrude set up the plan that Edward would fire the gun only when she called, "ATEOORD"?

3. Why do you think Trudy said, "Bergm op Zoom!" when she pointed at Edward in the last paragraph?

4. How do you think Edward felt about the possibility of killing someone with a gun (before he shot the Indians)? How do you think he felt just after he killed the Indians? How do you think he felt as an adult?

5. Would you like to fire a matchlock gun? Why or why not?

ACTIVITIES

1. Look up more information about the Van Alstynes.

2. Make up a tune to go with the Dutch song. Sing it in Dutch and English.

3. Pretend you're a newspaper, radio, or television reporter. Write or give an oral report on Edward's experience.

ADAM OF THE ROAD

written by Elizabeth Janet Gray
illustrated by Robert Lawson
published by Viking, 1942

ABOUT THE BOOK

A traveling minstrel, his son, and a dog travel in England in 1294. After the dog is stolen, the three become separated. They search for several months before they are reunited.

FOR DISCUSSION

1. Why do you think someone as young as Adam was able to survive his adventure so well?

2. Which of Adam's adventures would you most and least like to share? Why?

3. Contrast minstrels to today's entertainment.

4. How have food and sleeping arrangements changed from then to now?

5. What methods could be used if Adam were separated from his father today?

ACTIVITIES

1. Write instructions for the game "Tilting at the Quintain"; then play.

2. Put on your own minstrel show.

3. Draw a map of their travels. Make Adam's route one color, Roger's a different color, and Jankin's another color.

JOHNNY TREMAIN

written by Ester Forbes
illustrated by Lynd Ward
published by Houghton Mifflin, 1943

ABOUT THE BOOK

Thirteen-year-old Johnny becomes involved in the events leading to the Revolutionary War. He witnesses the Boston Tea Party and the Battle of Lexington.

FOR DISCUSSION

1. What role does Johnny's burned hand play in the story?

2. Was Johnny a good apprentice? Why or why not?

3. What famous people are mentioned in the book? What did you learn about them that you didn't know before?

4. What did the book teach you about the Revolutionary War?

5. Would you have liked to live during the Revolutionary War? Why or why not?

ACTIVITIES

1. Read a famous speech or document from that time aloud.

2. Give an oral or written report of one of the famous people mentioned in the book.

3. Draw a map of the places mentioned in the book. Include a small drawing to represent the places.

1945

RABBIT HILL

written and illustrated by Robert Lawson
published by Viking, 1944

ABOUT THE BOOK

When people move into a long-empty house, the woodland creatures of Rabbit Hill wonder if the people will plant a garden. The animals learn the new people love animals, for they plant enough for everyone.

FOR DISCUSSION

1. Why do you think the "new folks" moved to Rabbit Hill?

2. What are some good and bad things about rabbits? Why are they good? Why are they bad?

3. In what ways is the book contrary to nature? (An example is that the animals can read.)

4. Do you know any people with the same personality traits as the animals mentioned? Do animals have separate personalities? Why or why not?

5. Compare and contrast real rabbits with cartoon rabbits such as Bugs Bunny.

ACTIVITIES

1. Sample "rabbit food" (lettuce, carrots, etc.).

2. Write a report on some aspect of rabbits (food, breeds, superstitions, etc.).

3. Observe a rabbit for several days. How much does it eat? How much of a garden could it destroy?

STRAWBERRY GIRL

written and illustrated by Lois Lenski
published by Viking, 1945

ABOUT THE BOOK

A family moves to Florida to become small crop farmers. Through determination, the family endures strawberry crop failure and troublesome neighbors.

FOR DISCUSSION

1. Do you think the Boyers were "uppity" when they met the Slaters for the first time? Why or why not?

2. Why do you think each of the Slaters acted the way he or she did?

3. Why do you think the organ was so important to Birdie?

4. Would you have gone to help the Slaters if they treated you like they treated the Boyers? Why or why not? Why do you think Mrs. Boyer went over to help them?

5. What are some good and bad qualities neighbors have?

ACTIVITIES

1. Do a good deed for a neighbor. (Examples: rake/mow lawn, shovel sidewalk, walk a dog, etc.)

2. Plant strawberries and study how they grow.

3. Bake and/or eat something made out of strawberries.

MISS HICKORY

written by Carolyn Bailey
illustrated by Ruth Gannett
published by Viking, 1946

ABOUT THE BOOK

Miss Hickory has apple twigs for a body and a hickory nut for a head. An unwelcome guest forces her from her home. Her friends suggest new places to live, but she eventually becomes part of an apple tree.

FOR DISCUSSION

1. How do you think Miss Hickory came to be "alive"?

2. Why do you think Miss Hickory was friendly with the animals?

3. What other places could have been a good home for Miss Hickory?

4. What would have been a better ending for Miss Hickory's head?

5. Do you think Ann will make another Miss Hickory? Why or why not?

ACTIVITIES

1. Make a doll similar to Miss Hickory. Include clothes made from leaves, etc.

2. Learn about grafting plants and experiment with grafting yourself.

3. Draw a picture or build a model of a good home for Miss Hickory.

THE TWENTY-ONE BALLOONS

written and illustrated by William Pene du Bois
published by Viking, 1947

ABOUT THE BOOK

Professor Sherman sets out to cross the Pacific Ocean in a balloon in 1833. He spends time on the enchanting island of Krakatoa until the island is destroyed. Only his knowledge of balloons saves the people.

FOR DISCUSSION

1. In his Newbery acceptance speech, the author said he was mean to make Professor Sherman speak in front of a crowd. Why is it difficult to make a speech?

2. Would you like to live on Krakatoa? Why or why not?

3. What other inventions like the automatic sheet washer and electric living room can you think of?

4. If you had all those diamonds available to you, would you sell many of them at once to live a very comfortable life-style? Why or why not?

5. Would you like to ride in a balloon? Why or why not?

ACTIVITIES

1. Make a model of a balloon.

2. After your teacher has assigned you a letter, make up a restaurant menu with a type of food starting with that same letter, e.g. A – American, B – British, C – Chinese, etc.

3. See how many times you can pass a balloon from one to another without catching it or letting it touch the ground.

1949

KING OF THE WIND

written by Marguerite Henry
illustrated by Wesley Dennis
published by Rand McNally, 1948

ABOUT THE BOOK

A foal is born with a "wheat ear" sign on its chest which foretells evil. A mute stableboy saves the foal from being destroyed and names him Sham. Eventually Sham's speed earns him the name of "The Godolphin Arabian." Many racehorses even today are descended from Sham.

FOR DISCUSSION

1. Should animals (horses, in this case) observe the same religious rules (fasting) as their owners? Why or why not?

2. What were some of the superstitions surrounding Sham?

3. Why do you think Agba felt so strongly about the foal?

4. What purpose does Grimalkin serve in the book?

5. How would the book be different if Agba could talk?

ACTIVITIES

1. Trace the bloodline of a famous horse as far back as you can go.

2. Invite a horse trainer, jockey, or other person who works with horses to speak.

3. Rewrite a scene from the book with Agba speaking with others.

THE DOOR IN THE WALL

written and illustrated by Marguerite de Angeli
published by Viking, 1949

ABOUT THE BOOK

Wartime conditions and the plague in thirteenth-century England force a noble family to send their crippled son Robin away from his home. Robin eventually finds a way to help the king even without going to battle.

FOR DISCUSSION

1. What disease do you think Robin had? Why?

2. How would you pass the time if you were confined to bed?

3. How do you think Robin's lameness helped his courage?

4. In what ways does Brother Luke help Robin? Why do you think Brother Luke spends so much time helping Robin? How does Robin help Brother Luke?

5. What would you like and dislike about living in Robin's time? Why?

ACTIVITIES

1. Research the causes and treatment of crippling diseases.

2. Build a castle out of sugar cubes.

3. Learn to whittle. Start with a bar of soap and a nonserrated butter knife.

AMOS FORTUNE, FREE MAN

written by Elizabeth Yates
illustrated by Nora A. Unwin
published by Aladdin, 1950

ABOUT THE BOOK

Amos Fortune was born a prince in Africa. He was brought to the United States to be a slave. He worked his way to freedom and also helped other slaves become free again.

FOR DISCUSSION

1. Amos was born a prince, then became a slave. How do you think other slaves would have treated Amos if they knew? Why?

2. Why do you think people in that time felt that owning another human being was OK?

3. How would you react if someone speaking a foreign language kidnapped you, put you in shackles, and forced you to be a slave?

4. What were Amos' good qualities? Bad traits? Would you like to have Amos for a friend? Why or why not?

5. Did Amos deserve to be free and gain the freedom of others? Why or why not?

ACTIVITIES

1. The author decided to write the story of Amos after she had seen the graves of him and his wife. Go to a cemetery and make a charcoal rubbing of an old tombstone.

2. Research tanning methods. Try a variety of experiments on a piece of leather or chamois.

3. Write to the Chamber of Commerce in East Jaffrey, New Hampshire, and request information on Amos Fortune.

GINGER PYE

written and illustrated by Eleanor Estes
published by Harcourt, 1951

ABOUT THE BOOK
Jerry and Rachel search for their dog Ginger. The dog was stolen on Thanksgiving Day and found several months later.

FOR DISCUSSION
1. Rachel and Jerry don't like "I" books (those written in first person). Do you prefer books written in first, second, or third person? Why?

2. Do you know anyone who has an aunt or uncle younger than he or she? Would you like to have an aunt or uncle younger than you? Why or why not?

3. Was Ginger worth the work Rachel and Jerry had to do to earn the money to buy her? Why or why not?

4. What other things could Rachel and Jerry have done to find Ginger?

5. Why do you think Uncle Bennie recognized Ginger but Gramma didn't?

ACTIVITIES
1. Pretend your pet or an animal from a favorite book or television show is lost. Write a "Lost and Found" ad for the newspaper.

2. Search for a pet or inanimate object that you or someone else has lost.

3. Invite an animal trainer or obedience school teacher to speak. Then work to train your pet or one belonging to a friend.

1953

SECRET OF THE ANDES

written by Ann Nolan Clark
illustrated by Jean Charlot
published by Viking, 1952

ABOUT THE BOOK

An Incan boy learns his cultural history and the skill of keeping llamas. Discontented, he leaves his valley, but returns to take a sacred vow to guard the Inca's gold and to keep the llama herd intact.

FOR DISCUSSION

1. If you were Cusi, would you want to see more of the world than Hidden Valley? Why or why not?

2. Do you think Cusi was happy living with Chuto? Why or why not?

3. What do you think Cusi's biological family was like? Why do you think Cusi was abandoned?

4. Why do you think the beggar refused the corn Cusi offered him?

5. Would you like to take care of llamas? Why or why not?

ACTIVITIES

1. Find out if any farmers or ranchers in your area raise llamas. Invite one to speak, or find out if you could visit the farm.

2. After your teacher sets up a bartering system in the classroom, assigns an equal number of a variety of different questions and answers to a few students, and gives each of the other students the same amount of "money" (poker chips, play money, or slips of paper with values printed on them), you and your fellow students barter for the questions and answers.

3. Tell or write a description of a truck as if you were explaining it to someone who's never seen or heard of one.

...AND NOW MIGUEL

written by Joseph Krumgold
illustrated by Jean Charlot
published by Crowell, 1953

ABOUT THE BOOK

Twelve-year-old Miguel wishes to join the men when they take the sheep to the summer pastures. He works hard to learn about the sheep and learns about himself in the process.

FOR DISCUSSION

1. Why is being the middle child difficult? The oldest child? The youngest? An only child? What's good about being in each of those positions?

2. Would you like to take care of sheep? Why or why not? What would be the best thing about it? The worst?

3. Would you like to go on the journey to take the sheep to the mountains? Why or why not?

4. What concerns and fears would you have for a brother who was joining the army?

5. What would you do if you fell into a fleece bag? What kind of thoughts would you have? Describe the physical and emotional surroundings.

ACTIVITIES

1. Visit a petting zoo or sheep ranch to see and touch sheep. If no sheep are available, obtain raw wool to feel, and compare to finished wool.

2. Hold a class fiesta.

3. Research wool and make a list of all the things that wool can be used for.

THE WHEEL ON THE SCHOOL

written by Meindert DeJong
illustrated by Maurice Sendak
published by Harper, 1954

ABOUT THE BOOK

School children from a Dutch village attempt to lure storks to nest on the rooftops. Soon, the entire community is involved. Children and adults alike learn to work together.

FOR DISCUSSION

1. Would you like to go to a school with only six students? Why or why not?

2. Would you like to be the only girl (or boy) in a classroom? Why or why not? What would the advantages and disadvantages be?

3. Why was having storks nesting on the roof so important to Lina? To the other villagers?

4. Would you work as hard as the children in this story to lure storks to your village? Why or why not?

5. How did Janus help the children? How did the children help Janus?

ACTIVITIES

1. Build a model wheel using rolled-up newspaper.

2. Build or supply a birdhouse for the birds in your area.

3. Write an essay similar to Lina's about a different bird.

CARRY ON MR. BOWDITCH

written by Jean Lee Latham
illustrated by John O'Hara Cosgrave, II
published by Houghton Mifflin, 1955

ABOUT THE BOOK

Nathaniel Bowditch is indentured to serve on a clipper ship when he is only 12-years-old. He teaches himself and studies the stars until he is able to write a navigation guide that is still used today.

FOR DISCUSSION

1. How would you feel if you were indentured? What would be the advantages and disadvantages of working like that?

2. Why do you think Nat worked so hard on his studies when it wasn't required?

3. Why do you think Nat was driven to write a book about navigation?

4. How do you think people first learned to use stars for navigation?

5. How has navigation changed since Nat's day? What do you think Nat would think about radar and other electronic methods of navigation?

ACTIVITIES

1. Read (or try to read) passages from *The American Practical Navigator*.

2. Study constellations and/or visit a planetarium.

3. Use rubber bands to fasten dark tissue paper over a flashlight lens. Use a straight pin or small nail to make holes in the paper corresponding to stars in a constellation. Turn off the overhead light and shine the flashlight on a blank wall or the ceiling.

1957

MIRACLES ON MAPLE HILL

written by Virginia Sorensen
illustrated by Beth and Joe Krush
published by Harcourt, 1956

ABOUT THE BOOK

A troubled family moves to the country for a year. While there, they learn how to work together to help those around them while helping themselves.

FOR DISCUSSION

1. How would you try to help your father if he was a prisoner of war? Another relative or friend? A stranger?

2. What were the advantages and disadvantages of living on Maple Hill? Why?

3. Why do you think the father began to relax more and more the longer he lived on Maple Hill?

4. How did the Chrises help Marly and Joe? Mother and Father? How were the Chrises helped in return?

5. Name all the "miracles" and why they were miracles.

ACTIVITIES

1. Make a list of things made with maple flavoring. Taste as many as possible.

2. Make maple leaf prints. Lay a maple leaf (real or cut from construction paper) in the center of a piece of construction paper. Dip a toothbrush into very thin paint or ink. Use a small twig to pull the bristles of the brush toward you. The ink or paint will splatter around the leaf. Remove the leaf. Leave the center blank, or use the space to record information about trees or yourself, a recipe using maple flavoring, etc.

3. Study the properties of trees. Find out why leaves change colors, etc.

RIFLES FOR WATIE

written by Harold Keith
no illustrations
published by Crowell, 1957

ABOUT THE BOOK

Sixteen-year-old Jeff joins the Union Army during the Civil War. He learns that both sides have valid reasons for fighting after he is captured by the Confederate Army.

FOR DISCUSSION

1. Would you like to have been a soldier during the Civil War? Why or why not?

2. Would you have supported the Union or Confederate side? Why? Which side do you think the author would have supported? Why?

3. How did Jeff's rapport with animals help him? How would the book have been different if he hadn't liked animals?

4. How did Jeff change throughout the book?

5. The author interviewed several Civil War veterans for his research. How would speaking with someone who experienced the war instead of just reading about the war help a writer?

ACTIVITIES

1. Make a timeline and map of Jeff's travels.

2. List the pros and cons for both the Union and Confederate sides of the Civil War.

3. The author changed the lives of several generals in the book. Select one of the generals to research, and list the differences.

1959

THE WITCH OF BLACKBIRD POND

written by Elizabeth George Speare
no illustrations
published by Houghton Mifflin, 1958

ABOUT THE BOOK
Kit is a happy-go-lucky girl living in Barbados in the late 1600s. She's sent to live with Puritanical relatives in Connecticut. She finds the life difficult and befriends a woman known as "the witch."

FOR DISCUSSION
1. What do you think Kit found most difficult in her new life? Why?

2. Why do you think Kit and the witch became friends?

3. What is your opinion on the Puritan view of religion? The home? School? Girls? Punishments? How are today's views different? The same?

4. Why do you think people are intolerant of someone different from them?

5. How have you and others you know treated someone who looked, spoke, believed, or acted differently than you? Why? What would you like to do differently next time? Why? The same? Why?

ACTIVITIES
1. Make a list of several of the superstitions in the book. Tell why you think they were started.

2. Research hornbooks and make a replica of one.

3. Make a list of "crimes and punishments" for the classroom. (Examples: Chewing gum – bring a piece for each of the other students. Forgetting homework – do an extra report.)

ONION JOHN

written by Joseph Krumgold
illustrated by Symeon Shimin
published by Crowell, 1959

ABOUT THE BOOK

Onion John is an eccentric old man. The Rotary Club tries to transform Onion John's way of life. A young boy is the only one who seems to understand that Onion John prefers his life as it is.

FOR DISCUSSION

1. Why do you think Andy was able to understand Onion John better than anyone else?

2. Why do you think Onion John felt more at ease in a messy room?

3. Onion John used bathtubs for storage rather than for washing. What other things could bathtubs be used for?

4. What hazards could modern houses contain to someone unfamiliar with them? (For example, Onion John didn't fully understand the kitchen stove which resulted in a fire.)

5. Why did Andy consider himself lucky? Do you consider yourself lucky or unlucky? Why?

ACTIVITIES

1. Make a class recipe book of things made from onions. Sample as many as possible.

2. Make a list of the valuables you have that you'd like to take with you to a new home.

3. Start or become involved with a community project. (For example, clean up litter.)

1961

ISLAND OF THE BLUE DOLPHINS

written by Scott O'Dell
no illustrations
published by Houghton Mifflin, 1960

ABOUT THE BOOK
An Indian girl spends eighteen years alone on an island. In her struggles to survive, Karana learns about nature and herself.

FOR DISCUSSION
1. Why do you think Karana dived into the water and swam back to shore to her brother?

2. Why do you think Karana finally became friends with the leader of the dogs instead of killing him?

3. What are some of the customs Karana broke? What if she had refused to break them?

4. The book is based on a true story. How much of the book do you think the author invented, and how much do you think was fact? Why?

5. Do you think a wild animal such as a wolf or bear would make a good pet? Why or why not?

ACTIVITIES
1. Write a diary of happenings pretending you spent a week by yourself on an island.

2. Make tools and weapons the way Karana made them.

3. Read the sequel to the book *Zia*.

THE BRONZE BOW

written by Elizabeth George Speare
no illustrations
published by Houghton Mifflin, 1961

ABOUT THE BOOK

A Jewish boy in biblical times longs for freedom from the Romans. He's torn between joining the outlaw Rosh or following Simon the Zealot.

FOR DISCUSSION

1. Was Daniel right in wanting revenge against the Romans? Why or why not?

2. Rosh was an outlaw, yet he was kind to Daniel. Were you surprised? Why or why not?

3. Why do you think Daniel changed his way of thinking throughout the book?

4. Which characters are you most and least like? Why?

5. Would you have liked to live in biblical times? Why or why not?

ACTIVITIES

1. Make a bulletin board mural of the events in the book.

2. Find Bible passages that support events in the book.

3. Write a description of Daniel's character traits as he is at the beginning of the book. Then write another description of him at the end of the book. Compare the two for differences and similarities.

1963

A WRINKLE IN TIME

written by Madeleine L'Engle
no illustrations
published by Farrar, 1962

ABOUT THE BOOK

With the help of a friend, Meg and Charles Wallace search for their scientist father in the fifth dimension. Three mysterious women show them how to find him.

FOR DISCUSSION

1. Why do you think Calvin fit in so well with the Murrys?

2. How would you try to help Meg feel better about herself?

3. Would you like to live on Camazotz? Why or why not?

4. Where would you like to "tesser" to? Why?

5. In what ways can you show love?

ACTIVITIES

1. Practice bouncing balls and/or skipping rope in unison.

2. Select an object and explain to Aunt Beast the difference between what it looks like and what it is like.

3. Read these sequels: *A Wind in the Door*, *A Swiftly Tilting Planet*, and *Many Waters*. Characters from these books also appear in minor roles in many of Madeleine L'Engle's other books.

IT'S LIKE THIS, CAT

written by Emily Neville
illustrated by Emil Weiss
published by Harper, 1963

ABOUT THE BOOK

A teenager in New York City talks to his cat to ease his troubles. Cat leads the boy to two new friends — a girl his own age and a troubled older boy.

FOR DISCUSSION

1. Why do you think Dave got a cat instead of a dog like his father had?

2. Why do you think Dave often "escaped" to Aunt Kate's?

3. Why do you think Tom Ransom picked the lock to help Dave rescue the cat?

4. Why do you think the tension between Dave and Pop made Mom's asthma worse?

5. Is "Cat" a good name? Why or why not? What would you name the cat?

ACTIVITIES

1. Write a letter to an animal (your pet or a character from TV, movies, or a book) and thank it for helping you through a rough time.

2. Make a collage of cats (drawn, cut from magazines, or a combination).

3. Make a list of pros and cons for owning a dog, then for owning a cat. Compare lists of those who own dogs, cats, both, and neither.

1965

SHADOW OF A BULL

written by Maia Wojciechowska
illustrated by Alvin Smith
published by Atheneum, 1964

ABOUT THE BOOK
The son of a famous bullfighter is expected to follow in his father's footsteps. Manolo doubts his courage but finally has the opportunity to prove himself.

FOR DISCUSSION
1. Do you think Manolo was a coward? Why or why not?

2. Would you like to fight bulls? Why or why not?

3. Do you agree with many animal rights activists who say bullfighting is inhumane? Why or why not?

4. How would it be easier or harder to be the child of someone famous? Why?

5. Should children be expected to enter the same profession as their parents? Why or why not?

ACTIVITIES
1. Make a list of the professions you would like to enter. Tell why you chose them and how likely you are to actually do them.

2. Practice the various cape passes mentioned in the glossary.

3. Act out bullfighting, taking turns being the bull and the matador.

I, JUAN DE PAREJA

written by Elizabeth Borton de Trevino
no illustrations
published by Farrar, 1965

ABOUT THE BOOK
Juanico is the Negro slave to the painter Velazquez. Through the help of the painter, the slave becomes a painter and a free man.

FOR DISCUSSION
1. Do you think Juan was wrong in secretly painting when law forbade slaves to practice the arts? Why or why not?

2. Why do you think Juan felt the urge to paint?

3. Would you enjoy working for Velazquez? Why or why not?

4. Was Velazquez right in writing the letter of manumission before answering the king? Why or why not?

5. Would you have rather lived in Spain or Italy during that time? Why?

ACTIVITIES
1. Look for reproductions of Velazquez and Juan's paintings in art books.

2. Paint or draw a series of illustrations to go with the book.

3. Experiment with the primary colors (red, blue, and yellow). Make charts of what colors they make when mixed in different formulas.

1967

UP A ROAD SLOWLY

written by Irene Hunt
no illustrations
published by Follett, 1966

ABOUT THE BOOK

After her mother's death, Julie goes to live with an austere aunt. As a teenager, Julie chooses to stay with the aunt since the other people in her life seem to have allowed others to take her place.

FOR DISCUSSION

1. How did Julie's feelings for each of her family members change throughout the book?

2. How do you think Julie felt when Laura and Bill named their baby after her? Would you like a niece or nephew named after you? Why or why not? Would you like to be named after an aunt or uncle? Why or why not?

3. Was Aunt Cordelia a good aunt? Why or why not? Was Uncle Haskell a good uncle? Why or why not?

4. Do you think Uncle Haskell was a good writer? Why or why not? Why do you think he didn't pursue writing more?

5. What other things could have happened in Aunt Cordelia's past that weren't mentioned in the book?

ACTIVITIES

1. Write an epilogue about the rest of Julie's life.

2. Decorate a "room" made out of a box tilted on its side. Then redecorate it in a completely different style.

3. Pretend you're graduating. Write and/or give a speech.

FROM THE MIXED-UP FILES OF MRS. BASIL E. FRANKWEILER

written and illustrated by E.L. Konigsburg
published by Atheneum, 1967

ABOUT THE BOOK

Claudia takes her brother with her to the Metropolitan Museum of Art in New York City, where they hide for a week. To pass the time, they try to determine if a marble statue was actually sculpted by Michelangelo.

FOR DISCUSSION

1. Do you think Claudia had good reasons for running away? Why or why not?

2. Was Jamie a good choice as a "running away partner"? Why or why not?

3. Why do you think Claudia was so fascinated by the statue?

4. Do you like the title of the book? Why or why not? What other titles would be good?

5. What is your favorite part of a museum? Why? Least favorite? Why?

ACTIVITIES

1. Look for pictures of Michelangelo's art in art books.

2. Visit a museum or create a classroom museum out of items brought by the students.

3. Plan how much money you would need to live for a week the way Claudia and Jamie did.

1969

THE HIGH KING

written by Lloyd Alexander
no illustrations
published by Holt, 1968

ABOUT THE BOOK
The assistant pig-keeper leads the quest to rescue the sword that symbolized the strength of the kingdom of Pyrdain. Taran becomes a hero in this final book of the Chronicles of Pyrdain.

FOR DISCUSSION
1. What kind of job would an assistant pig-keeper do today?

2. What kind of challenges would Taran face if the same story were set in the modern-day United States?

3. Do the unusual names add, detract from the story, or not make a difference? Why? What more familiar names could they be today?

4. Who is your favorite and least favorite character from the book? Why?

5. If you could shape-change, what would you want to change to? Why?

ACTIVITIES
1. Find other stories from Welsh mythology.

2. Compare the places in Prydain to Wales.

3. Read the four previous books in the series and the Prydain picture books.

SOUNDER

written by William H. Armstrong
illustrated by James Barkley
published by Harper, 1969

ABOUT THE BOOK

A black man is sentenced to a chain gang for stealing food during the Depression. His son searches for his father and his dog Sounder who was wounded during the arrest.

FOR DISCUSSION

1. Why do you think the deputy shot Sounder? Did he have a right? Why or why not?

2. What do you think the younger children thought of their father being away from home? Sounder's disappearance?

3. Why do you think the author didn't give the boy a name?

4. Why do you think the book the boy found in the trash meant so much to him? Would you be willing to walk eight miles each way to school like the boy did? Why or why not?

5. Why do you think Sounder was quiet until the father returned?

ACTIVITIES

1. The book is based on the life of one of the author's teachers. Write about an incident in your life that you feel deeply about.

2. Have each student pick a notable black American and give an oral report or write a report on him or her.

3. Practice sharecropping. Let your teacher be the landowner and you and your fellow students the sharecroppers. Use buttons, slips of paper, poker chips, etc., to represent crops. You "earn" your "crops" with good grades or other rewards. The "landowner" then takes his or her "share" from the supply.

SUMMER OF THE SWANS

written by Betsy Byars
illustrated by Ted CoConis
published by Viking, 1970

ABOUT THE BOOK
A teenage girl's outlook on life changes after her mentally retarded brother disappears in search of the swans.

FOR DISCUSSION
1. Was Aunt Willie a good guardian? Why or why not?

2. How do you think each of the family (Sara, Wanda, Charlie, Aunt Willie, Mr. Godfrey) felt about each of the others?

3. Why do you think Mr. Godfrey didn't come immediately when he found out Charlie was missing?

4. What if Charlie had a digital watch?

5. Why do you think Sara had difficulty apologizing to Joe?

ACTIVITIES
1. Read Hans Christian Andersen's *The Ugly Duckling* and compare it to Sara's story.

2. Visit swans at a zoo or other nature center, or write a report about swans. Find out if swans ever come to your area and when.

3. Invite a police officer to speak about the procedure for locating a lost child; then organize a search for a lost pet or inanimate object.

MRS. FRISBY AND THE RATS OF NIMH

written by Robert C. O'Brien
illustrated by Zena Bernstein
published by Atheneum, 1971

ABOUT THE BOOK

A group of laboratory rats is given human intelligence. They escape and establish their own community. A mouse named Mrs. Frisby seeks their help when one of her children becomes ill.

FOR DISCUSSION

1. Would you like to work at the laboratory NIMH? Why or why not?

2. Is the mouse family true to nature? Why or why not?

3. Why do you think the rats gave Dragon sleeping powder instead of poison?

4. Billy put Mrs. Frisby in a cage. Do you think it's fair to cage a wild animal? Why or why not? Is it right to use animals in laboratory experiments? Why or why not?

5. Why do you think the name "Mrs. Frisby" was changed to "Mrs. Brisby" in *The Secret of NIMH*, the movie version of the book?

ACTIVITIES

1. Design a maze for mice or rats to travel through. If an animal is available, see how long it takes it to get through the maze. Try the experiment several times and compare the results.

2. Draw a map of the rats' movements from the Farmers' Market to Thorn Valley.

3. Find out more about NIMH (National Institute of Mental Health).

1973

JULIE OF THE WOLVES

written by Jean Craighead George
illustrated by John Schoenherr
published by Harper, 1972

ABOUT THE BOOK

An Eskimo girl runs away from her husband. On her journey across the
Alaskan tundra, she befriends a pack of wolves. Finally, she must decide
whether to return to civilization or remain on her own.

FOR DISCUSSION

1. Julie was 13 when she married. Is that too young? Why or why not?

2. Should parents be allowed to choose who and when their children should
marry? Why or why not?

3. Do you think Julie would have been happy living with the wolves for the
rest of her life? Why or why not?

4. Would you like to live with wolves for a time? Why or why not? Would you
have the knowledge to survive?

5. Discuss survival techniques you would use if you became lost. (Mark a
trail, carry a garbage bag with you for protection from the elements, etc.)

ACTIVITIES

1. Watch a pet, wild animal, or bird for several weeks. Keep notes of its
routine. See if you can recognize what it "says."

2. Give an oral or written report on Alaska, Eskimos, or wolves.

3. Divide into groups. The first group blazes a trail. (The "trail" could be a
series of signs scratched in the dirt or drawn with chalk on the cement in the
school yard.) The next group tries to follow the signs.

THE SLAVE DANCER

written by Paula Fox
illustrated by Eros Keith
published by Bradbury, 1973

ABOUT THE BOOK

A boy is kidnapped to play his fife aboard a slave ship. Jessie's sympathy for the slaves turns to hatred until the ship is destroyed. Jessie and a black boy are the only survivors and must learn to work together.

FOR DISCUSSION

1. Why do you think Jessie was curious about the slaves even before his experiences on the slave ship?

2. Why do you think Jessie grew to hate the slaves? Was it the slaves' fault? Why or why not?

3. Do you think Jessie would have been content to stay with Daniel until he was grown? Why or why not?

4. Why do you think Jessie grew up to fight on the Union side of the Civil War even though he was from New Orleans?

ACTIVITIES

1. On a map of the world, follow the approximate route that Jessie took.

2. Read a copy of the Emancipation Proclamation.

M.C. HIGGINS THE GREAT

written by Virginia Hamilton
no illustrations
published by Macmillan, 1974

ABOUT THE BOOK

A black boy daydreams from the top of a shiny forty-foot pole. He learns about his family, heritage, and himself when a mud slide threatens the family.

FOR DISCUSSION

1. How would the Higgins' lives have changed if Banina had become a singing star?

2. Should Lurhetta have told M.C. that she didn't know how to swim? Why or why not? Should he have asked her if she could swim? Why or why not?

3. What purpose do the Killburns play in the story?

4. What things could the Higgins do to escape the danger of the mud slide?

5. The book closes on their building a wall under threatening skies. What do you think happens? Is there a mud slide? Why or why not?

ACTIVITIES

1. Research strip mining, and tell how it damages nature and what can be done.

2. Pretend you're atop M.C.'s pole. Write a few paragraphs on what you were thinking about.

3. Role-play Lurhetta and M.C. as if she called him on the telephone one month after the book ends.

THE GREY KING

written by Susan Cooper
illustrated by Michael Heslop
published by Atheneum, 1975

ABOUT THE BOOK

A boy moves to his uncle's farm in Wales to regain his health. He battles the Grey King, an enemy from the dark, with the help of an albino and a dog.

FOR DISCUSSION

1. What do you think made the car jump and hit the rock that destroyed the tire? Why do you think the scene had to take place?

2. Why do you think Bran was known as "the raven boy"? Was that a good nickname for him? Why or why not?

3. How could you "see the wind"?

4. Why do you think Gwen, Bran's mother, left him?

5. Why do you think Wales is a common setting for fantasy novels? (*The High King* is also set in a mythical Wales.)

ACTIVITIES

1. Find and read some of the King Arthur legends.

2. Read the other books in the "Dark is Rising" series.

3. Make a mobile or collage of significant items from the book (harp, dog, tire, etc.).

ROLL OF THUNDER, HEAR MY CRY

written by Mildred Taylor
no illustrations
published by Dial, 1976

ABOUT THE BOOK

A black family in Mississippi struggles to live and retain their pride during the Depression. Cassie, brought up to be independent, finds the prejudices especially difficult.

FOR DISCUSSION

1. Would you give your coat to T.J.? Why or why not?

2. Who would you rather have for a friend – Cassie or Lillian Jean? Why?

3. Was Mrs. Logan a good teacher? Why or why not?

4. Why do you think T.J. associated with R.W. and Melvin? Why do you think they associated with T.J.?

5. Why do you think Papa burned the cotton even if T.J. still had to go to jail?

ACTIVITIES

1. Write the incident between Cassie and Lillian Jean at the store from Lillian Jean's point of view.

2. Try to "count the states" as Cassie did in chapter 11.

3. Books were cherished gifts in the Logan household. Find out what you can do to get books to children who can't afford them.

BRIDGE TO TERABITHIA

written by Katherine Paterson
illustrated by Donna Diamond
published by Crowell, 1977

ABOUT THE BOOK

The Burkes move into the old Perkins Place. They don't fit in well with the community; their house is full of books, yet they don't have a television. Leslie Burke and Jess Aarons become friends and create the kingdom of Terabithia. One day Leslie drowns on her way to Terabithia.

FOR DISCUSSION

1. What would you name your secret world? Why?

2. What would you give a special person if you didn't have any money?

3. Miss Edmunds was considered to be a hippie. What do you think a hippie is? Why do you think someone labeled a hippie was often disliked?

4. Should Jess have invited Leslie to go to Washington with him and Miss Edmunds? Why or why not?

5. Should Jess have invited his sisters to Terabithia after Leslie's death? Why or why not?

ACTIVITIES

1. Listen to a recording and/or sing the songs the students sang with Miss Edmunds in chapter 2.

2. Write about or draw Terabithia and/or your own secret world.

3. Leslie didn't have television to watch. Go for one week without turning on the television. Make a list of what you do instead of watching TV.

THE WESTING GAME

written and illustrated by Ellen Raskin
published by Dutton, 1978

ABOUT THE BOOK

A girl sneaks into the Westing Mansion and discovers the body of Samuel Westing. His will states that the ones who solve a riddle he provided will inherit the Westing fortune.

FOR DISCUSSION

1. Do you know anyone like any of the characters in the book? Why are they alike? How are they different? Which character is most like you? Why?

2. Which character would you like to be paired with? Why? Which would you least like to be paired with? Why?

3. Would you like to try to solve a similar riddle to inherit a fortune? Why or why not? Would you like to do it just for fun? Why or why not?

4. What would you do with the $10,000 given to you for solving the riddle?

5. Was Sam Westing smart to devise the plan he did? Why or why not?

ACTIVITIES

1. Draw or build a model of Sunset Towers in a cutaway view. Show where everyone lived.

2. Make up a puzzle, riddle, secret code, logic puzzle, or scavenger hunt for your friends to try to solve.

3. Mark lines on a fat candle and record the time it takes for the candle to burn to each line.

A GATHERING OF DAYS: A NEW ENGLAND GIRL'S JOURNAL 1830-32

written by Joan W. Blos
no illustrations
published by Scribner, 1979

ABOUT THE BOOK

A girl keeps a diary of an eventful two years in her life. Her father bringing home a stepmother and stepbrother, seeing a runaway slave, and experiencing the death of a friend are only a few of her entries.

FOR DISCUSSION

1. Would you help the "phantom"? Why or why not?

2. Do you think using newspapers and other nontextbooks in the classroom is a good idea? Why or why not?

3. Why do you think the mention of Cassie's death is broken off in the middle of a sentence then enclosed in bold black lines?

4. Do you think Aunt Lucy had a girl or a boy? What do you think they named the baby?

5. Did you enjoy the journal format of the book? Why or why not? Do you prefer straight prose? Why or why not?

ACTIVITIES

1. Begin keeping your own journal. It doesn't have to be fancy – many journals have been kept on backs of envelopes.

2. Collect food and clothing for the needy as a class project.

3. Find out more about the Underground Railroad which helped slaves escape to the North.

JACOB HAVE I LOVED

written by Katherine Paterson
no illustrations
published by Crowell, 1980

ABOUT THE BOOK
A tomboy growing up in the 1940s is jealous of her pretty and talented twin sister. Louise befriends a "heathen" who helps her obtain her goal of becoming a nurse midwife.

FOR DISCUSSION
1. Did Louise have a right to be jealous of Caroline? Why or why not? Should Caroline have been jealous of Louise? Why or why not?

2. Why do you think Louise and Call became and remained friends?

3. Should Louise have sent the $25 to Lyrics Unlimited to have her poem made into a song? Why or why not?

4. Did Louise and Caroline pick a good way to get rid of the cats? Why or why not?

5. Why do you think Louise was content to be a nurse midwife instead of a doctor? Should she have tried harder to become a doctor? Why or why not?

ACTIVITIES
1. Find out the difference between identical and fraternal twins. Invite sets of each to the class to answer questions.

2. Write a poem or song as if you were going to send it to Lyrics Unlimited.

3. Sample seafood such as, crabs, oysters, clams, etc. If you live in a coastal area, learn to catch your own seafood, or watch someone who does.

A VISIT TO WILLIAM BLAKE'S INN

written by Nancy Willard
illustrated by Alice and Martin Provensen
published by Harcourt, 1981

ABOUT THE BOOK

"Blake's Celestial Limousine" takes the narrator to an inn managed by William Blake. Poems tell of the dragons who bake bread and other fanciful creatures, until the great poet himself is introduced.

FOR DISCUSSION

1. Would you like to visit the Inn? Why or why not?

2. Could you sleep easily if you were using a bear for a pillow? Why or why not?

3. If you had to share a room with one of the characters in the book, which one would you choose? Why? Which one(s) wouldn't you like to share with? Why?

4. Why do you think William Blake gave the rat a handful of dirt but gave everyone else stars?

5. What story would you tell the tiger? Why?

ACTIVITIES

1. Write a poem about another possible mythical guest or employee of the Inn.

2. Draw or paint a picture to go with your poem.

3. Read some of William Blake's poetry.

1983

DICEY'S SONG

written by Cynthia Voigt
no illustrations
published by Atheneum, 1982

ABOUT THE BOOK

In this sequel to *Homecoming*, Dicey tries to adjust to living with her grandmother. After her mother dies, Dicey finally begins to break the shell around her.

FOR DISCUSSION

1. Why do you think Dicey put so much time and effort into the boat?

2. How are Dicey and Mina alike and different?

3. Why do you think Gram's children, Liza and John, lost contact with Gram?

4. Do you think being financially forced to cremate Liza worked out well? Why or why not?

5. Why do you think the book was titled *Dicey's Song*?

ACTIVITIES

1. Read the first related book, *Homecoming*, and other books by Cynthia Voigt to find out more about the characters.

2. Pretend you are given $100 to buy gifts for Gram, James, Sammy, Maybeth, and you. Use a catalog or visit stores to make a list of what you would buy. Use as much of the money as possible without going over the limit.

3. Do the assignment Dicey's class did. Write a character sketch of someone you know. Then write a character sketch of yourself.

1984

DEAR MR. HENSHAW

written by Beverly Cleary
illustrated by Paul O. Zelinsky
published by Morrow, 1983

ABOUT THE BOOK

A troubled boy begins writing letters to his favorite author. Mr. Henshaw encourages Leigh to start a diary. The diary reveals his concerns about school and his parents' divorce.

FOR DISCUSSION

1. Why do you think Leigh chose Mr. Henshaw as the one to tell his innermost secrets? Was Mr. Henshaw a good choice? Why or why not?

2. Why do you think Leigh's father didn't call more often? Why was the jacket a good gift for Leigh?

3. Why do you think Mr. Fridley is so understanding of Leigh's problems? Why do you think Leigh didn't go to him for more help?

4. Would you like to have lunch with an author? Why or why not? Was a writing contest a good method of choosing who would be able to attend the lunch? Why or why not?

5. Why do you think Leigh told his father to keep Bandit?

ACTIVITIES

1. Answer the questions Mr. Henshaw asked Leigh.

2. Find out more about the background of a favorite author. Read and reread the author's books. Write to the author in care of his or her publisher.

3. Start keeping a journal to try to understand what's going on in your life.

1985

THE HERO AND THE CROWN

written by Robin McKinley
no illustrations
published by Greenwillow, 1984

ABOUT THE BOOK

Aerin tries to win the people's trust. She sets out to gain the Hero's Crown. Aerin must battle a dragon and an evil mage in the process.

FOR DISCUSSION

1. Why do you think the king's horse didn't fall after being wounded? Why do you think Aerin felt such a kinship with Talat?

2. How do you think the others in the castle felt about Aerin? Why? About Galanna? Why?

3. Why were people prejudiced against Aerin from the start (female, born of a witch woman, etc.)? Would Aerin encounter the same prejudices today? Why or why not?

4. Why do you think Aerin felt compelled to fight the dragon? To seek the man she dreamed about? To face Agsded and get the Crown?

5. Why do you think the author once compared the battle with the dragon to living in an urban slum?

ACTIVITIES

1. Draw or make a three-dimensional model of a dragon.

2. Make up recipes for the unfamiliar foods mentioned in the book (mikbars, malak, saha jam, etc.). Make a class book out of the recipes. Sample the goodies, of course!

3. Find information on dragons and compare it with the dragon in the book.

SARAH PLAIN AND TALL

written by Patricia MacLachlan
no illustrations
published by Harper, 1985

ABOUT THE BOOK
A mail-order bride moves in with the family. They grow to love Sarah, but she misses her old home. When Sarah takes the wagon to town one day, the family becomes concerned that she will not return.

FOR DISCUSSION
1. Is mail order a good way to find a wife/stepmother? Why or why not?

2. What would you like to know about a mail-order bride before you meet her? (Does she sing, braid hair, etc.?)

3. Why do you think Sarah added, "Do you have opinions on cats? I have one."

4. Why do you think Papa threw his cut hairs to the birds behind the barn?

5. Do you think Sarah will visit Maine again someday? Why or why not? If yes, do you think she would take any of her new family along or would she rather go alone? Why?

ACTIVITIES
1. Search for bird nests with hair woven in them. Be sure not to disturb any birds or eggs.

2. Write an ad for a newspaper advertising for a spouse. Vote for the one you would like to respond to.

3. Find out if anyone in your community knows anyone who is or married a mail-order bride.

THE WHIPPING BOY

written by Sid Fleischman
illustrated by Peter Sis
published by Greenwillow, 1986

ABOUT THE BOOK

It's unlawful to spank a prince in Jemmy's land. Jemmy is taken from the orphans to receive the punishments Prince Brat deserves. Jemmy finds himself enmeshed in a dangerous plan surrounding Prince Brat.

FOR DISCUSSION

1. Why do you think the prince was so naughty?

2. Why do you think Jemmy learned how to read, write, and do sums, but the prince didn't?

3. Why do you think the prince got so bored he ran away? Why do you think the king asked to be included the next time the boys ran away?

4. Why do you think Jemmy changed his mind about the prince and told the hot-potato man, "We left my friend behind"?

5. Do you think a prince has a right to have someone else take his punishment for him? Why or why not? Would you like someone else to take punishment for you? Why or why not?

ACTIVITIES

1. Switch roles with someone (parent, sibling, friend, teacher, etc.) for a specified length of time, including duties and responsibilities.

2. Scratch a letter to a friend using a feather and homemade ink made from berries or other items.

3. Figure out how much money you'd have if you had your weight in gold. (Current gold prices are listed in most major newspapers.)

LINCOLN: A PHOTOBIOGRAPHY

written by Russell Freedman
illustrated with photographs
published by Clarion, 1987

ABOUT THE BOOK

Lincoln's boyhood, young manhood, and political career are featured in this biography. Many samples of Lincoln's writings are included.

FOR DISCUSSION

1. What do you admire most and least about Lincoln? Why?

2. Why do you think Lincoln usually looked solemn and dignified in his photographs and paintings? Did they reflect his true personality? Why or why not?

3. Did Mary Todd make a good wife for Lincoln? Why or why not?

4. Do you agree with Lincoln's political policies? Why or why not?

5. Would Lincoln be a good president today? Why or why not?

ACTIVITIES

1. Read Lincoln's speeches aloud the way he probably read them.

2. Write for more information about the Lincoln Historical Sites.

3. Find other quotations by Lincoln.

1989

JOYFUL NOISE: POEMS FOR TWO VOICES

written by Paul Fleischman
illustrated by Eric Beddows
published by Harper, 1988

ABOUT THE BOOK
This collection of insect poems is meant to be read aloud by two readers at once. Each poem centers around a particular insect in fact and/or fantasy.

FOR DISCUSSION
1. Why do you think the author chose to write poems about insects?

2. What is your favorite insect (not necessarily in the book)? Why? Is there a poem for it? If so, do you like the poem? Why or why not? If not, why do you think the insect wasn't included?

3. Do you like the humorous or serious poems better? Why?

4. Is it difficult to read the poems silently? Why or why not? How does hearing them read aloud in two voices affect them?

5. Why do you think the book is titled *Joyful Noise*? Do you like the title? Why or why not?

ACTIVITIES
1. Select an insect (not necessarily one from the book) and give an oral or written report about it.

2. Listen to Bach's "Two-Part Inventions." Compare and contrast the music with the poems.

3. Try writing your own two-part poems. An easy way to start is with a question/answer format or comparison. Possible subjects could be doctors and nurses, cats and dogs, flowers and weeds, etc. You could also try three-part poems. Possible subjects include children/parents/grandparents and water/air/land.

NUMBER THE STARS

written by Lois Lowry
no illustrations
published by Houghton Mifflin, 1989

ABOUT THE BOOK

Ten-year-old Annamarie and her family help a Jewish family escape from Nazi soldiers in Copenhagen to the safety of Sweden.

FOR DISCUSSION

1. What do you think would have been the worst thing about living in Denmark in 1943? Why? The best? Why?

2. Why do you think Jewish people were persecuted?

3. Why do you think Uncle Henrik helped the Jewish people escape?

4. What did Kirsti add to the story? Why?

5. Where would you have hidden Ellen's necklace? Why?

ACTIVITIES

1. Read similar books of Jewish persecution during World War II such as *The Diary of Anne Frank* and *The Upstairs Room* by Johanna Reiss.

2. Get a baby picture from each member of the class. Try to match each picture with the student.

3. Kirsti received shoes made from fish skin. Draw a picture or make a three-dimensional model of "fish shoes" – the more outrageous the better.

MANIAC MAGEE

written by Jerry Spinelli
no illustrations
published by Little, Brown, 1990

ABOUT THE BOOK

Jeffrey, a runaway better known as Maniac, has remarkable athletic ability and courage. The white boy finds a home with a black family until reverse racism forces him to find a new home.

FOR DISCUSSION

1. Which of Maniac's activities do you think are impossible? Why? Which do you think are possible but not probable?

2. Would you like a friend like Maniac? Why or why not?

3. Do you think "Maniac" is a good nickname for Jeffrey? Why or why not? Would you like that nickname? Why or why not?

4. In which of Maniac's "homes" (the home of his aunt and uncle, that of the Beales, the zoo, the Band Shell, the home of the McNabs, etc.) would you most like to live? Why? Least? Why?

5. In what ways can people be considered to be members of a minority group? (Consider race, religion, gender, age, etc.)

ACTIVITIES

1. Take a survey of nicknames in the classroom. Take note of those without nicknames, and those who have nicknames from first names, last names, physical features, etc. Who (parent, sibling, friend, etc.) gave each person his or her nickname?

2. Find a book on macramé or nautical knots and learn to tie knots.

SHILOH

written by Phyllis Reynolds Naylor
no illustrations
published by Atheneum, 1991

ABOUT THE BOOK

Marty Preston finds a mistreated dog that belongs to Judd Travers, a neighbor who starves and beats his hunting dogs. Marty hides Shiloh and struggles with his conscience over the theft. Finally he comes to a solution: trading work for ownership of the dog.

FOR DISCUSSION

1. Why do you think Judd Travers is cruel to his dogs?

2. Do you think that 20 hours of work was a fair price for Shiloh? Why or why not?

3. Where would you hide a dog like Shiloh? Why?

4. What kind of pet would you most like to own? Why? How would you convince your parents to let you have this pet?

5. What would you do if you knew someone was mistreating an animal? Why?

ACTIVITIES

1. Visit the local Humane Society or invite someone from the ASPCA or Humane Society to speak to the class.

2. Research the hunting laws in your area (opening date of season, firearm restrictions, etc.).

3. Build a maze for animals and insects. Judge each animal on its speed and on its ability to adapt to the maze.

MISSING MAY

written by Cynthia Rylant
no illustrations
published by Orchard/Richard Jackson, 1992

ABOUT THE BOOK

Summer has been raised by her aunt and uncle since she was six. When her Aunt May dies, Summer both grieves for her aunt and worries about her uncle, who still senses May's presence.

FOR DISCUSSION

1. Ob and May didn't have much money, but they gave Summer a great deal of love. Do you think Summer would have been happier if she had more material things? Why or why not?

2. Ob said May's spirit was near even after her death. Do you believe in spirits? Why or why not?

3. Would you like Cletus for a friend? Why or why not?

4. Cletus wanted to visit the Capitol. If you could go anywhere you wanted, where would you go? Why?

5. Why do you think Ob decided to put his whirligigs in May's garden?

ACTIVITIES

1. Design and make a whirligig out of heavy paper.

2. Cletus is a collector. Select something that you would like to collect. Tell the class why you chose your collection and how you will store it.

3. Pick out a picture from a box or can label and make up a story to go with it.

THE GIVER

written by Lois Lowry
no illustrations
published by Houghton Mifflin, 1993

ABOUT THE BOOK

Jonas lives in a future time in a utopian community. He is selected to be the receiver of past knowledge. He learns about war, disease, and other disasters, but also about the positive aspects of past civilizations, such as music and color. Jonas eventually flees the utopian community in search of a better life.

FOR DISCUSSION

1. Name some situations in which rules can be different in different places (such as in school—different teachers may have different rules). What are some rules in your family that may be different in other families?

2. What would you like to do when you have finished with school for good. Why? What do you think your Assignment at Twelve would be? Why?

3. Would you like living in a society as structured as Jonas's? Why or why not? What would be the advantages and disadvantages of living in such a society?

4. As the Giver gave Jonas snow, what one experience or object would you like to be able to transmit to others if they had not experienced it? Why?

5. What memory would you least like to give up forever? Why? Which one would you most like to give up? Why? Would you choose the same memories if they were to be given to others? Why or why not?

ACTIVITIES

1. Discuss dreams at the beginning of the class and feelings at the end of the class in much the same way that Jonas's family did at mealtimes.

2. Select a different job for each person in the class. Make a list of at least ten duties associated with each job.

3. Find a way to describe various colors to someone who has never before seen colors. You may use words, actions, objects, sounds, or any other method as long as the colors themselves are not used as part of the description.

NOTES & UPDATES

ANIMALS OF THE BIBLE

text selected by Helen Dean Fish
illustrated by Dorothy P. Lathrop
published by Lippincott, 1937

ABOUT THE BOOK
Illustrations accompany the selections of text from the King James version of the Old and New testaments of the Bible.

FOR DISCUSSION
1. Which animal is your favorite in the illustrations? Why? In the text? Why?

2. Which animal do you like the least in the illustrations? Why? In the text? Why?

3. Do you think you'd like the illustrations more or less if they were in color? Why?

4. Why do you think Helen Dean Fish chose the Bible for selections of text?

5. What other animals would you like to see mentioned and illustrated?

ACTIVITIES
1. Memorize a verse or series of verses from the text.

2. Search for more references to animals in the Bible.

3. Draw a picture or series of pictures about a day in the life of one animal.

MEI LI

illustrated and written by Thomas Handforth
published by Doubleday, 1938

ABOUT THE BOOK
Mei Li, her brother, their dog, and a thrush encounter a variety of adventures when they attend the New Year's Day Fair in Peking.

FOR DISCUSSION
1. How is the fair Mei Li attended different and alike from those you've attended?

2. Which of Mei Li's adventures is your favorite? Why?

3. Would you like a thrush for a pet? Why or why not?

4. What unusual customs did the characters have (e.g., bowing to the poultry)?

5. What are your New Year's Day customs?

ACTIVITIES
1. Divide the class into groups to put on a "fair." Groups could be acrobats, fortune-tellers, pitch-penny coordinators, etc.

2. Tell or write a story as if Mei Li went to a modern-day fair in your area.

3. Sample Chinese food. (Fortune cookies are a simple and inexpensive sample.)

ABRAHAM LINCOLN

written and illustrated by Ingri and Edgar d' Aulaire
published by Doubleday, 1939

ABOUT THE BOOK
The biography of Abraham Lincoln begins with his birth in a log cabin and ends at the conclusion of the Civil War.

FOR DISCUSSION
1. What do you like best and least about Lincoln? Why?

2. What new things did you learn about Lincoln?

3. Do you know anything about Lincoln the book doesn't mention?

4. Do you think Lincoln was a good president? Why or why not?

5. Would Lincoln be a good president today? Why or why not?

ACTIVITIES
1. Read the book on or near Lincoln's birthday, February 12. Make a suitable birthday card for him.

2. Make pencil rubbings of Lincoln pennies. Secure pennies to a table or piece of cardboard with a loop of tape. Place a piece of lightweight paper over the pennies. Rub a pencil, charcoal, chalk, or crayon lightly over the pennies. Do a different design by varying the number and spacing of the pennies.

3. Make a stovepipe hat out of black construction paper. Make a beard with yarn. Tie loops in the ends of a length of yarn to fit over your ears. Tie additional strands of yarn to a long piece of yarn for the beard.

1941

THEY WERE STRONG AND GOOD

written and illustrated by Robert Lawson
published by Viking, 1940

ABOUT THE BOOK
Robert Lawson tells of his ancestors which include a sea captain, a soldier, and frontier women. Their qualities prove that they were "strong and good."

FOR DISCUSSION
1. Which of the author's ancestors is your favorite? Why? Least favorite? Why?

2. Does any one person in the book remind you of someone you know? If yes, why?

3. What do the pictures tell you in addition to the text?

4. What are the important events in people's lives (births, marriages, moving, etc.)? What stories have you heard about your own ancestors?

5. What do you think your children and grandchildren will be able to say about you?

ACTIVITIES
1. Make a complete family tree with names and dates.

2. Make a collage sculpture from items of various family members. Items could include a lone earring, leftover pieces from a model car, bent nails, etc.

3. Talk to a parent or grandparent and find out more about your ancestors — what jobs they had, where they lived, and a special story about them. For example: "My father was born near McClusky, North Dakota. He was a farmer for thirty years; then he bought apartment buildings and became a landlord. When he was about 7-years-old, he was playing by a plow and broke his leg. His sister was spanked for not watching him closely enough."

MAKE WAY FOR DUCKLINGS

written and illustrated by Robert McCloskey
published by Viking, 1941

ABOUT THE BOOK

Mrs. Mallard leads her family through Boston's city streets to the pond in the Public Garden. Their journey is aided by a policeman who stops traffic for them.

FOR DISCUSSION

1. Do you think people would be willing to wait for the ducks to cross streets today? Why or why not?

2. Could the ducks have made the journey without the help of the policeman? Why or why not?

3. Why do you think the ducks walked instead of flew?

4. The author originally wanted to do the story about pigeons, but he found ducks easier to draw. Would the story be as fun if the characters were pigeons? Why or why not?

5. When Robert McCloskey was illustrating the book, he kept ducks in his bathtub. Would you like to do that? Why or why not?

ACTIVITIES

1. Visit ducks at a zoo or farm.

2. Hold "duckwalk" races. "Run" in a squatting position with your fingers under your arm as "wings."

3. Trace the approximate route of the ducks on a Boston map. Then trace a possible route on a local map for a duck family to go from one place to another.

1943

THE LITTLE HOUSE

written and illustrated by Virginia Lee Burton
published by Houghton Mifflin, 1942

ABOUT THE BOOK

The little house begins in the country and survives many seasons. Eventually a city grows up around it and the house is moved back to the country.

FOR DISCUSSION

1. What hardships do buildings have to endure (weight of snow on roofs, rain, wind, etc.)?

2. A city grew up around the little house. Many people would consider that progress. Is progress good for everyone? Why or why not?

3. One of the effects of progress is pollution. What kinds of things can we do to stop or at least slow down pollution?

4. If you could move your house, where would you move it, if at all? Would you like to move into a different house? Why or why not?

5. What are the advantages and disadvantages of living in the city? In the country?

ACTIVITIES

1. Choose an old building in your city and research the changes it's gone through over the years.

2. Divide into groups; make replicas (by drawing or out of boxes) of the little house. Each group should make a different part of the little house's life (new, one of the seasons, surrounded by the city, being moved, old, etc.).

3. Keep a daily journal of the changes in the seasons. Sample entries could be about the amount of snowfall or how many leaves are left on the trees, etc.

MANY MOONS

written by James Thurber
illustrated by Louis Slobodkin
published by Harcourt, 1943

ABOUT THE BOOK

A princess demands the moon. Her father requests the help of his royal staff. Each one fails until the royal jester lets the princess solve her own problem.

FOR DISCUSSION

1. What if the king simply said, "No, you can't have the moon," to his daughter?

2. What would you do if the king asked you to get the moon for the princess?

3. James Thurber, the author of the book, eventually became blind. How would you describe the moon to a blind person? What could you give a blind person to feel to give him or her an idea of what the moon is like?

4. What would the author and characters have thought about the "moon landing" in 1969?

5. What have we learned about the moon since 1943, the year the book was published?

ACTIVITIES

1. Make a model of the earth and moon. Show how the moon circles the earth. Using a flashlight, show how the moon can be seen only in phases.

2. Follow the phases of the moon for at least one month.

3. Put on a play of the story *Many Moons*.

1945

PRAYER FOR A CHILD

written by Rachel Field
illustrated by Elizabeth Orton Jones
published by Macmillan, 1944

ABOUT THE BOOK
A child's prayer asks for blessings for a variety of items including toys, food, and people.

FOR DISCUSSION
1. What is your favorite toy, dish, piece of furniture, etc.? Why?

2. Do you ever recite a memorized prayer? How often? Do you ever make up your own prayers? Which do you think is better? Why?

3. What are some other things in the illustrations but not in the text that the girl could be thankful for?

4. What other things not mentioned in the book are you thankful for?

5. Would a boy be thankful for the same things in the book the girl is? Why or why not?

ACTIVITIES
1. Study a religion different than yours or invite someone to talk about different religions.

2. Make a list of all the things you are thankful for.

3. Bring your favorite toy, dish, etc., to school and tell the class or write a paragraph about why it's your favorite.

THE ROOSTER CROWS

selected and illustrated by Maud and Miska Petersham
published by Macmillan, 1945

ABOUT THE BOOK

A variety of well-known and lesser-known nursery rhymes, jump-rope chants, and folk-jingles are gathered in this collection.

FOR DISCUSSION

1. Are any of the jingles in the book different than the way you've heard them before? How?

2. What new jingles did you hear?

3. What's your favorite and least favorite entry in the book? Why?

4. What other jingles do you know that could be added to the book?

5. How are the jingles similar to "rap" music? Different?

ACTIVITIES

1. Pick a different jingle (from the book or one you know) and make an illustration (drawing, painting, collage, etc.) for it. Compile the illustrations into a class book.

2. Divide into groups. Each group should recite or act out a few of the jingles in the book.

3. Select an entry in the book and translate it into modern-day language.

THE LITTLE ISLAND

written by Golden MacDonald
illustrated by Leonard Weisgard
published by Doubleday, 1946

ABOUT THE BOOK
A kitten visits an island and learns about the changes of the plant and animal life there during the day and night, the seasons, and a storm.

FOR DISCUSSION
1. Would you like to visit the island? Why or why not? Live there? Why or why not?

2. What is your favorite and least favorite aspect of the island? Why?

3. What would you do with your time if you were stranded on the island?

4. What would you like to build on the island, if anything?

5. The island was patterned after an island off the northeastern coast of the United States. How would the story be different if it were set in another part of the world?

ACTIVITIES
1. Select a plant or animal and find out more about it.

2. Build your own island. Place a rock in the center of a pan of water. Add cutout or toy figures of trees, animals, etc.

3. Make a list of things you recognize as the change in seasons. For example, colder temperatures indicate fall or winter, seeing the first robin indicates spring, etc.

WHITE SNOW, BRIGHT SNOW

written by Alvin Tresselt
illustrated by Roger Duvoisin
published by Lothrop, 1947

ABOUT THE BOOK
A wide range of adults and children experience different reactions to a major snowfall.

FOR DISCUSSION
1. Do you know of anyone who has the same reaction as the people in the book to snow? Why?

2. Which character in the book are you most and least like? Why?

3. Do you like snow? Why or why not?

4. What games and other activities can you do in the snow that can't be done without snow? What games and activities can't be played in the snow?

5. For those who have seen snow, how would you describe snow to someone who hasn't seen it? For those who haven't seen snow, what do you think snow is like?

ACTIVITIES
1. Cut a snowflake design out of folded paper.

2. Paint a picture of snow falling on a dark background. Use a cotton swab or pencil eraser dipped in white paint for the snowflakes.

3. Study how snowflakes are formed.

1949

THE BIG SNOW

written and illustrated by Berta and Elmer Hader
published by Macmillan, 1948

ABOUT THE BOOK
The animals start to prepare for winter, but an unexpected snowfall catches them unprepared. Two kind people come to their rescue.

FOR DISCUSSION
1. What's your favorite and least favorite animal in the book? Why?

2. What do you do to prepare for winter?

3. What kinds of activities do you enjoy in winter? What do you dislike about winter?

4. What can you do to help animals get through winter?

5. What animals do you see in summer but not in winter? Where are they during the winter?

ACTIVITIES
1. Set up a bird feeder. A simple feeder can be made from a plastic cup. Tie a knot in a string and pull the string through the bottom of the cup. Smear peanut butter on the cup, then roll in birdseed. Hang the cup by the string.

2. Study hibernation, migration, etc.

3. Make a frost picture. Mix equal amounts of Epsom salts and boiling water. Let cool. Use a paintbrush to dab solution across a drawn or cutout picture. Let dry.

SONG OF THE SWALLOWS

written and illustrated by Leo Politi
published by Scribner, 1949

ABOUT THE BOOK

The gardener of the Mission San Juan Capistrano teaches a boy about the swallows that return each spring. The man and boy work together to make a garden for the birds.

FOR DISCUSSION

1. Why do you think Juan and Julian are friends?

2. Why do you think the swallows return each spring and leave each fall?

3. How do baby birds act when they're learning to fly?

4. Would you like to visit San Juan Capistrano? Why or why not?

5. Is there a place in your area similar to the gardens of San Juan Capistrano? In what ways are they similar and different?

ACTIVITIES

1. Play and/or sing the song included at the end of the book.

2. Find out the days the swallows arrive and depart from San Juan Capistrano each year.

3. Keep a bird diary. Write down the birds you see in the school yard each day.

1951

THE EGG TREE

written and illustrated by Katherine Milhous
published by Scribner, 1950

ABOUT THE BOOK
After Katy and her brother hunt for Easter eggs, Grandmom teaches them how to decorate the eggs and make an egg tree.

FOR DISCUSSION
1. What are your Easter traditions, if any?

2. Why do we celebrate Easter?

3. What are some good places to hide (or look for) Easter eggs?

4. Can rabbits lay eggs? Why or why not?

5. Would you like to decorate Easter eggs to sell or show at craft fairs? Why or why not?

ACTIVITIES
1. Create your own design and name it similar to those in the book. Examples from the book are: "The Bright and Morning Star" and "The Deer on the Mountain."

2. Make your own egg tree. Prick a hole in each end of several eggs. Blow out the insides. Paint the eggshells and hang them from tree branches placed in a bucket of sand.

3. Hunt for Easter eggs hidden by the teacher. The "eggs" can be paper, marbles, wrapped candy, etc.

FINDERS KEEPERS

written by William Lipkind
illustrated by Nicholas Mordvinoff
published by Harcourt, 1951

ABOUT THE BOOK
Two dogs find a bone and argue about who should have it. A farmer, the barber, and a goat can't help them. A big dog finally teaches them a lesson in sharing.

FOR DISCUSSION
1. What would you tell the dogs if they asked you which one should have the bone?

2. Who's the smartest character in the book? Why? In what ways are the other characters smart?

3. How could the dogs have used the hay from the farmer? The advice from the goat? The hair from the barber?

4. Do you think the dogs were happy with sharing the bone? Why or why not?

5. What things aren't meant to be shared (homework, silverware, etc.)?

ACTIVITIES
1. Conduct a study in randomization. Divide into groups. Flip a coin 100 times and keep a record of the number of "heads" and "tails." Compare the results of each group.

2. Play "pin the bone in the dog's mouth." Make two identical dogs that face each other and label them "Nap" and "Wrinkle." Each child should cut out an identical paper bone and print his or her name on it. Blindfold each other and try to pin the bone in a dog's mouth.

3. Make a bone mobile. Hang one clothes hanger from the bottom of another. You may want to tape them together to keep them from sliding. Hang a cutout of a dog in the center and cutouts of various colored bones around the dog.

1953

THE BIGGEST BEAR

written and illustrated by Lynd Ward
published by Houghton Mifflin, 1952

ABOUT THE BOOK

Johnny decides to get a bearskin for the barn so it will be like all the other barns in the valley. He goes hunting for "the biggest bear," but returns with a live bear cub he makes into a pet.

FOR DISCUSSION

1. Would you like a bear for a pet? Why or why not?

2. What else could they have done to solve the problems the bear caused?

3. What would be a good name for a pet bear? Why?

4. Do you think Johnny could have shot the bear? Why or why not?

5. Would you have liked to live in the days when bears were more common? Why or why not?

ACTIVITIES

1. Finger-paint bears using chocolate pudding as "paint."

2. Serve treats fit for a bear. Mix equal parts of peanut butter and honey and add raisins if you wish. Smear the mixture on apple wedges.

3. Find recent articles about bear sightings in and around cities.

MADELINE'S RESCUE

written and illustrated by Ludwig Bemelmans
published by Viking, 1953

ABOUT THE BOOK

A dog named Genevieve is banished from a boarding school in Paris after the girls quarrel over her ownership. The dog returns with a solution to the problem – puppies.

FOR DISCUSSION

1. Would you like to live with Madeline and the other girls? Why or why not?

2. Why do you think the girls live there? Orphanage? Boarding school?

3. How would you have solved the problem of arguing over the dog?

4. Do you think the dog was given fair treatment by being banished? Why or why not? What else could they have done with her?

5. What kind of dog is Genevieve? Would you like to have one like her? Why or why not?

ACTIVITIES

1. Describe what a day in Madeline's school would be like in words and/or pictures.

2. Research dogs and find out the average number of puppies in a litter. Would there be enough to go around to all the girls?

3. Find Paris on a map. Look through a travel guide to learn about Paris.

1955

CINDERELLA, OR THE LITTLE GLASS SLIPPER

translated and illustrated by Marcia Brown
published by Scribner, 1954

ABOUT THE BOOK

Thanks to a fairy godmother, a mistreated girl is able to attend the Royal Ball. She loses her glass slipper as she leaves. The prince searches for the owner and finally finds Cinderella.

FOR DISCUSSION

1. How is this version different from any others you've heard? The same?

2. Why do you think the stepsisters didn't recognize Cinderella?

3. Do you think the carriage, horses, footmen, etc., looked anything like their original form? Why or why not?

4. What else could the fairy godmother have used to make the carriage, footmen, etc., as if they had been only half-transformed?

5. Would you forgive your stepsisters as readily as Cinderella? Why or why not?

ACTIVITIES

1. Draw pictures of the carriage, footmen, etc., as if they had been only half-transformed.

2. Compare the shoes of everyone in the classroom. How many sneakers, sandals, loafers, laced shoes, etc., are there? How do the colors compare?

3. Conduct a short "ball" with classical music.

FROG WENT A-COURTIN'

retold by John Langstaff
illustrated by Feodor Rojankovsky
published by Harcourt, 1955

ABOUT THE BOOK
A variety of animals and insects attend the wedding feast of Frog and Miss Mousie. An uninvited guest, a cat, arrives and breaks up the party.

FOR DISCUSSION
1. What's your favorite and least favorite character? Why?

2. Why do you think the author chose a mouse and a frog as the wedding couple?

3. How do you think the wedding guests feel about each other?

4. Do you think Frog and Miss Mousie will have a happy marriage? Why or why not?

5. How do you think the cat broke up the party?

ACTIVITIES
1. Play the song at the end of the book. Make up your own verses.

2. Act out a wedding ceremony.

3. Draw a picture of other animals that could have been invited to the wedding.

A TREE IS NICE

written by Janice May Udry
illustrated by Marc Simont
published by Harper, 1956

ABOUT THE BOOK

The author tells a few of the many good things about trees. Included, among others, are the change of seasons, picking apples, burning leaves, and sitting in the shade.

FOR DISCUSSION

1. What other nice things are there about trees? Not-so-nice things?

2. What's your favorite and least favorite kind of tree? Why?

3. Why do you think there's a day devoted to trees (Arbor Day)?

4. Why do you think many places have laws against burning leaves?

5. Would you like to live in an area that has more, less, or the same number of trees than where you currently live? Why?

ACTIVITIES

1. Plant a tree – either a sapling or seeds. Fruit seeds (apple, orange, lemon, etc.) usually grow well with the proper care.

2. Make a tree bulletin board. Write the name of your class ("Ms. Smith's First Grade") on the trunk. Color and cut out one or more leaves and write your name on the front. Pin the leaves on and under the tree.

3. Collect leaves and identify them.

TIME OF WONDER

written and illustrated by Robert McCloskey
published by Viking, 1957

ABOUT THE BOOK
Island nature is revealed in the tides, changing seasons, and the force of a hurricane.

FOR DISCUSSION
1. The book is written in second person ("you" do things). Do you prefer first person ("I" do things), second person, or third person ("he or she" did things)? Why?

2. The people knew a storm was coming. What weather superstitions do you know?

3. What do you do to prepare for a storm? What do you do during a storm?

4. Where do you think hummingbirds (and other animals) go when it storms?

5. Would you like to live on that island? Why or why not?

ACTIVITIES
1. Read a section of the book aloud. Then read the same section again substituting a name for "you." Read the same section substituting "I" for "you."

2. The first hurricane of the year is given a name that starts with "A," the second "B," etc. All hurricanes used to be given girls' names. Now they alternate girls' names and boys' names. Make a list of names you would use. Obtain the actual list from the weather bureau and compare the two.

3. Too many things were described in the book to make a picture of each. Select one and draw a picture of it.

1959

CHANTICLEER AND THE FOX

adapted and illustrated by Barbara Cooney
published by Crowell, 1958

ABOUT THE BOOK
A sly fox slips into a chicken yard. He attempts to lure the rooster for his next meal. The rooster soon learns not to trust the fox's flattery.

FOR DISCUSSION
1. Why do you think the rooster trusted the fox at the beginning?

2. How else could the rooster have gotten away from the fox?

3. How do you think the rooster will feel about anyone else he meets? Will he trust them?

4. Are you more like the rooster or the fox? Neither? Both? Why?

5. What can be done to keep a fox or other predator away from chickens?

ACTIVITIES
1. Barbara Cooney chose to retell Chaucer's story about Chanticleer because she wanted to draw chickens. Draw a picture of whatever you would like to draw. Tell or write a remembered or made-up story about your picture.

2. Divide into groups of two – one to be the fox and one to be the rooster. Act out the story without using words.

3. Read all or a portion of Chaucer's version of *Chanticleer* aloud to the class.

NINE DAYS TO CHRISTMAS

written by Marie Hall Ets and Aurora Labastida
illustrated by Marie Hall Ets
published by Viking, 1959

ABOUT THE BOOK
A Mexican girl named Ceci chooses a beautiful star-shaped pinata. She's upset when she realizes it must be broken. Ceci is comforted when the pinata becomes a new star in the sky.

FOR DISCUSSION
1. Would you like to celebrate Christmas like Ceci? Why or why not?

2. *Nine Days to Christmas* was written in 1959. How do you think the customs have changed since then?

3. What are your Christmas or Hanukkah customs? (Opening presents Christmas Eve or Christmas morning, when and if stockings are hung, when tree is set up, etc.)

4. What Christmas do you remember the best? Why?

5. How do you think Ceci could have gotten over her disappointment of the broken pinata if it hadn't gone into the sky?

ACTIVITIES
1. Make a pinata. Decorate a paper bag and fill with wrapped candies and fruit. Hang from a tree or the ceiling. Blindfold each other and take turns hitting it with a broom handle or other stick.

2. Draw a picture of a pinata or make a miniature one out of a paper bag.

3. Sample Mexican food.

1961

BABOUSHKA AND THE THREE KINGS

written by Ruth Robbins
illustrated by Nicholas Sidjakov
published by Parnassus Press, 1960

ABOUT THE BOOK
A Russian peasant woman refuses to accompany the wise men in their search for the Christ Child. The next morning, the woman is sentenced to spend eternity searching for Him.

FOR DISCUSSION
1. Would you have gone with the men? Why or why not?

2. How could the wise men have convinced her to follow them?

3. How would the story be different if Baboushka went with the wise men?

4. Why do you think Baboushka decided to search the next morning?

5. Do you like the unusual illustrations in the book? Why or why not?

ACTIVITIES
1. Baboushka brings gifts like Santa Claus does in the United States. Research other Christmas legends.

2. Make crowns similar to those the wise men wore.

3. Find Russia and Bethlehem on a map of the world. Trace a path between them.

ONCE A MOUSE

retold and illustrated by Marcia Brown
published by Scribner, 1961

ABOUT THE BOOK

A hermit rescues a mouse from a crow. He changes the mouse into a variety of other animals to save it from other dangers. The hermit finally changes the ungrateful tiger back into a mouse.

FOR DISCUSSION

1. What is a hermit? What are some other names that would describe the man in the book (wizard, magician, sorcerer, etc.)?

2. How else could the hermit have saved the mouse?

3. What animal would you like to be? Why?

4. What do you think might have happened if the tiger had been grateful to the hermit?

5. Do you think the hermit should have left the mouse as a mouse? Why or why not?

ACTIVITIES

1. Act out the story.

2. The illustrations are woodcuts. Illustrate a story you know (or make one up) using a variety of rubber stamps and ink pads. Another possibility is to cut designs in cork and use a stamp pad for printing.

3. Make a list of the advantages and disadvantages of being each animal in the book.

1963

THE SNOWY DAY

written and illustrated by Ezra Jack Keats
published by Viking, 1962

ABOUT THE BOOK
Peter spends the day experiencing the wonder and joy of new-fallen snow.

FOR DISCUSSION
1. What do you like best and least about snow? Why?

2. How do you think Peter learned to make snow angels, the snowman, etc.?

3. What else could Peter have played in the snow?

4. What happened to the snowball in Peter's pocket?

5. What ways do you keep warm outside in the winter?

ACTIVITIES
1. The illustrations were made with pieces of other materials (the mother's dress was oilcloth, etc.). Make a picture with a variety of cutout materials.

2. Play snow games even if there isn't any snow.

3. Make a snow scene. Use a baby food or other small jar with a tight-fitting lid. Attach a small figurine to the inside of the jar with waterproof glue. Let dry. Fill the jar with water. Add shavings from a white wax crayon. Replace lid with figurine attached. Apply more waterproof glue around the lid. Let dry. Turn jar upside down and shake gently to make it "snow."

WHERE THE WILD THINGS ARE

written and illustrated by Maurice Sendak
published by Harper, 1963

ABOUT THE BOOK

Max is sent to bed without supper. He travels to the land "where the wild things are" and becomes their king. After Max becomes lonely, he returns home to a thoughtfully prepared supper.

FOR DISCUSSION

1. What kind of mischief do you think caused Max to be sent to bed without supper?

2. Would you like to visit the wild things? Why or why not?

3. Where do you think the wild things live? Why?

4. The author originally wrote the book with "wild horses" instead of "wild things." Do you think the book would have been better or worse with horses? Why?

5. Do you think Max's mother forgave him? Why or why not?

ACTIVITIES

1. Make cookies or cupcakes and decorate them like wild things; then eat them.

2. Draw or paint a picture of what you think one or more wild things look like.

3. Make a wild thing mask. Cut eyeholes out of a paper bag. Decorate the bag with yarn and construction paper to make a wild thing.

1965

MAY I BRING A FRIEND?

written by Beatrice Schenk de Regniers
illustrated by Beni Montresor
published by Atheneum, 1964

ABOUT THE BOOK

A boy visits a friendly king and queen. On each visit, the boy takes a different animal visitor with him.

FOR DISCUSSION

1. Would you like to have been at each of the parties? Why or why not?

2. Which was your favorite and least favorite guest? Why?

3. Why do you think the king and queen kept inviting the child back?

4. How do you think it was possible for the child to bring all the animals? (Parents were zookeepers, etc.)

5. Who would you take to a party on each of the seven days? Why?

ACTIVITIES

1. Read the book once to hear the bouncing sounds and once to listen for the story.

2. Eat something different as a treat each day of a week. (Fruit, vegetables and dip, cake, cookie, candy, etc.)

3. Make a zoo bulletin board. Pick an animal to draw and label with your name. Make sure it is different from animals already done. The teacher can be the zookeeper at the center of the board.

ALWAYS ROOM FOR ONE MORE

adapted by Sorche Nic Leodhas
illustrated by Nonny Hogrogian
published by Holt, 1965

ABOUT THE BOOK
A man living in a small house invites people in to get out of the bad weather. The visitors build the man a bigger house in return for his kindness.

FOR DISCUSSION
1. Why do you think the MacLachlans shared their house?

2. Why do you think the others built them a new house?

3. Would the story have been as fun if it were written in prose instead of poetry? Why or why not?

4. Did you enjoy the Scottish words? Why or why not?

5. What do you like about the illustrations? Dislike?

ACTIVITIES
1. Translate a part of the book into your own dialect.

2. Practice talking in the Scottish dialect.

3. Draw a picture of a room that reflects your personality (sports equipment, stuffed animals, books, etc.). Place it on a bulletin board to make a "house." Or, make a three-dimensional room in a small box and fasten the boxes together to make a house.

1967

SAM, BANGS AND MOONSHINE

written and illustrated by Evelyn Ness
published by Holt, 1966

ABOUT THE BOOK
Sam tells many tall tales. She learns her lesson when Thomas nearly drowns while searching for a baby kangaroo Sam claimed to have.

FOR DISCUSSION
1. Why do you think Sam tells "moonshine"?

2. Do you think Sam believed her own moonshine? Why or why not?

3. Why do you think Thomas believed her?

4. What would be a good punishment for telling moonshine?

5. Do you think "Moonshine" is a good name for a gerbil? Why or why not?

ACTIVITIES
1. Draw a picture of a gerbil and one of a kangaroo. How are they alike and different?

2. Sam's father said, "There's good MOONSHINE and bad MOONSHINE. The important thing is to know the difference." List several examples of good and bad moonshine.

3. Make up you own "moonshine" – the more outrageous, the better.

DRUMMER HOFF

adapted by Barbara Emberley
illustrated by Ed Emberley
published by Prentice-Hall, 1967

ABOUT THE BOOK

Each soldier brings a part of a cannon, then the powder, rammer, and the shot. Drummer Hoff fires it off in a splash of illustration.

FOR DISCUSSION

1. Which step in firing the cannon would you most like to do? Why? Least like to do? Why?

2. Which character do you like the best? Why?

3. Why do you think the illustration on the last page shows flowers growing around the cannon, spider webs, etc.?

4. Why do you think the book was written in poetry?

5. What do you like and dislike about the illustrations? Why?

ACTIVITIES

1. Act out the story keeping in time with who's reading.

2. Use drums to keep rhythm with someone reading the story. Use other instruments to indicate the different characters. Use cymbals to represent the cannon firing.

3. As a bulletin board idea, your teacher can place a cannon at one end of the board and label it with the name of the classroom or teacher. Place "self-portraits" (either drawn or photo with facts about you) so they look like cannonballs firing out of the cannon.

1969

THE FOOL OF THE WORLD AND THE FLYING SHIP

retold by Arthur Ransome
illustrated by Uri Shulevitz
published by Farrar, 1968

ABOUT THE BOOK
The fool makes many friends through kindness. These friends help him fulfill nearly-impossible tasks set by the czar. As a reward, the fool marries the czar's daughter.

FOR DISCUSSION
1. Is the "fool" really a fool? Why or why not?

2. Where would you look for a ship with wings?

3. Would you like to ride in a flying ship? Why or why not?

4. Do you think a contest to find a flying ship is a good way to select a husband? Why or why not?

5. What kindnesses have you done for people? What did you receive in return? What kindnesses have people done for you? What did you give them in return?

ACTIVITIES
1. Make paper airplanes and have contests for the prettiest, one that flies the farthest, one that stays afloat the longest, etc.

2. Do a good deed for someone every day for a set length of time. Keep a list of your good deeds.

3. Go on a class walk in search of items from a list (possibilities include a maple leaf, a red pebble, a feather, etc.).

SYLVESTER AND THE MAGIC PEBBLE

written and illustrated by William Steig
published by Windmill Books, 1969

ABOUT THE BOOK

Sylvester finds a pebble that grants wishes. He turns himself into a rock to escape a lion and cannot wish himself back. Through lucky coincidence, Sylvester's parents restore him.

FOR DISCUSSION

1. How would you escape a lion if you were in that situation? In what ways do animals adapt to their surroundings (hibernate, change color, etc.)?

2. What does being a family mean? How would your family feel if you were lost for months? What can be done to find a missing person?

3. Can a rock "think"? Why or why not?

4. Would you throw the pebble away after it caused the trouble? Why or why not?

5. People in the book are represented by various animals. What animal are you most like? Why? What animals are your friends and family most like? Why?

ACTIVITIES

1. Draw or paint a picture of what you'd wish for if you had a magic pebble.

2. Divide into groups of three. One of you should explain to the other two (the "parents") how you became a rock. The parents should respond with questions and/or comments.

3. Find a pebble and protect it for a week. Take it with you wherever you go. Keep notes of the problems you have with the responsibility.

1971

A STORY, A STORY

retold and illustrated by Gail E. Haley
published by Atheneum, 1970

ABOUT THE BOOK
Anase, the Spider Man, must capture a leopard, a hornet, and a fairy to pay for stories from the Sky God.

FOR DISCUSSION
1. Why do you think a spider man was a good choice as the main character?

2. Would you like to have the task of capturing the leopard, the hornet, and the fairy? Why or why not?

3. How else could Anase have trapped the leopard? The hornet? The fairy?

4. Would the story be as interesting if the author used more common names? Why or why not?

5. What would life be like if there weren't any stories to tell?

ACTIVITIES
1. Make a spider man out of construction paper and yarn.

2. Read other African legends and stories about Anase.

3. Cut a piece of dark construction paper to fit in the bottom of a round cake pan. Place a bit of paint in the center of the paper. Drop a marble in the pan. Tilt the pan back and forth so that the marble rolls through the paint to make a web.

ONE FINE DAY

adapted and illustrated by Nonny Hogrogian
published by Macmillan, 1971

ABOUT THE BOOK

A fox drinks a bucket of milk. An old woman cuts off his tail as punishment. She promises to sew it back on if he replaces the milk. One event leads to another as the fox travels to find the milk.

FOR DISCUSSION

1. Was the woman right or wrong in chopping off the fox's tail? Why?

2. How else could the fox have solved his problem?

3. Can a fox talk with people, a field, other animals, etc.? Why or why not?

4. What could have happened if one of the chain of events broke (for example, if a blue bead wasn't found)?

5. Can a fox's tail actually be sewn on after it's been removed? Why or why not? Would the fox be able to use his tail as he had before? Why or why not?

ACTIVITIES

1. Play "pin the tail on the fox."

2. Try to act out a title of a book, song, or common phrase without using words. The rest of the class can try to guess what it is.

3. Divide into groups and have procession races. (Each group should be given identical math or English problems.) The first child should do the first problem, the second should do the second, etc. The first group to correctly complete all the problems wins.

1973

THE FUNNY LITTLE WOMAN

retold by Arlene Mosel
illustrated by Blair Lent
published by Dutton, 1972

ABOUT THE BOOK
A Japanese woman is captured by the wicked oni who take her home to cook for them. After she becomes lonely, the woman escapes and takes a magical paddle with her.

FOR DISCUSSION
1. What are some other names that could be used for the oni? (Monsters, ogres, etc.)

2. Would you like to cook for the oni? Why or why not?

3. How would you have tried to escape the oni?

4. Why do you think the oni couldn't swim?

5. Was the woman wrong to steal the magic paddle? Why or why not?

ACTIVITIES
1. Experiment with regular and instant rice. Test the cost, taste, preparation time, cooked volume for same amount of uncooked, etc.

2. Make rice pictures. Glue rice to an outlined picture and paint.

3. Sample various things made from rice (rice cakes, cereal, fried rice, etc.).

DUFFY AND THE DEVIL

retold by Harve Zemach
illustrated by Margot Zemach
published by Farrar, 1973

ABOUT THE BOOK

Lazy Duffy brags about her spinning until the Squire takes her to spin for him. The Devil appears before Duffy and does her spinning. In exchange, she must tell him his name in three years or he will take her away.

FOR DISCUSSION

1. Would you make the same deal Duffy did? Why or why not?

2. What kind of person was Duffy? Would you like her for a friend? Why or why not?

3. What names would you guess? Why?

4. Why do you think the squire married Duffy?

5. Why do you think Duffy said she'd never knit another thing at the end of the book?

ACTIVITIES

1. Draw a picture of what you think the devil looks like if he doesn't look like the one in the book.

2. Make a list of all the words you don't know in the book and find out the meanings.

3. Read another version of Rumplestiltskin and compare and contrast it with this book.

1975

ARROW TO THE SUN

retold and illustrated by Gerald McDermott
published by Viking, 1974

ABOUT THE BOOK

An Indian boy leaves home to search for his father, the Sun. With the help of Arrowmaker, the boy finds his father, but the Sun refuses to accept him until he survives three tests.

FOR DISCUSSION

1. Why do you think the Boy's mother didn't tell him and his friends about his father?

2. Why do you think the Arrowmaker helped the Boy, but the Corn Planter and the Pot Maker didn't?

3. How do you think the boy was able to pass through the four chambers of ceremony?

4. What do you think someone with the Sun for a father would look and act like?

5. What do the illustrations tell that the story doesn't?

ACTIVITIES

1. Make pictures like those in the book. Cut out angular shapes and paste them on colored backgrounds.

2. Draw or make a picture of what you'd look like if you were turned into an arrow.

3. Research the Indian tribes in your area. If possible, invite a speaker to tell a few Indian legends.

WHY MOSQUITOES BUZZ IN PEOPLE'S EARS

retold by Verna Aardema
illustrated by Leo and Diane Dillon
published by Dial, 1975

ABOUT THE BOOK

Mosquito tells Iguana a lie which sets off a chain reaction of events that leads to disaster.

FOR DISCUSSION

1. What else could Iguana have done to keep from listening to the mosquito?

2. What kind of animals could have been used if the story were set in the United States?

3. What else could they have done to placate the owl?

4. What other sounds could have been used for the animals (instead of "mek, mek, mek" or "krik, krik, krik," etc.)?

5. Was everyone fair as to who was to blame? Why or why not?

ACTIVITIES

1. Play "gossip." Sit the class in a circle. Whisper a sentence into the first child's ear. That child should whisper it to the next child, etc. Each child should only be told once. The last child should say what he or she heard. Usually, the sentence is quite different from the original.

2. Watch the chain reaction of a row of dominoes when the first one is bumped.

3. Make a picture by gluing bits of cut or torn paper onto a background.

ASHANTI TO ZULU: AFRICAN TRADITIONS

written by Margaret Musgrove
illustrated by Leo and Diane Dillon
published by Dial, 1976

ABOUT THE BOOK
Costumes, homes, artifacts, and plant and animal life surrounding twenty-six African tribes are a few of the things depicted in words and pictures.

FOR DISCUSSION
1. Which tribe would you most like to be a part of? Why? Least like to be a part of? Why?

2. Would you like to visit Africa? Why or why not? Live there? Why or why not?

3. What do the illustrations tell that the text doesn't?

4. What surprised you the most in the book? What kinds of things did you learn?

5. How are African tribes like Indian tribes? Different?

ACTIVITIES
1. Find the areas mentioned on a map of Africa.

2. Ask your teacher to invite a speaker who has been to Africa or show a film of Africa.

3. Pick a tribe from the book or one that isn't mentioned and tell about a typical day as a member of the tribe.

NOAH'S ARK

translated and illustrated by Peter Spier
published by Doubleday, 1977

ABOUT THE BOOK

Only one page of text is included in this version of the familiar Bible story of the Ark: a translation of Jacobus Revius' poem "The Flood." The illustrations show the story of the ark.

FOR DISCUSSION

1. How do you know what Noah thinks or feels in each picture?

2. Do the pictures tell a story on their own, or would words help? Why?

3. If you didn't know the story of Noah, what else could the book be about?

4. Would you like to spend forty days and forty nights on an ark with all the animals? Why or why not?

5. Which animals are missing from the pictures?

ACTIVITIES

1. Assign a different animal to each student to talk or write about.

2. As a bulletin board idea, your teacher can make an ark for the center of the board. You can draw or paint a picture of a different pair of animals to be attached to the board.

3. Read the story of Noah's Ark from the Bible (Genesis 6-9).

THE GIRL WHO LOVED WILD HORSES

written and illustrated by Paul Gobel
published by Bradbury, 1978

ABOUT THE BOOK
Her love of horses drives a girl to try to calm them during a storm. The horses run away with her. She's rescued a year later but becomes ill until she returns to the horses.

FOR DISCUSSION
1. Would you like to be a horse? Why or why not?

2. Why do you think the girl's parents let her leave to live with the horses? If you were unhappy living with your parents, would they let you live with horses? Why or why not?

3. If you could be transformed into any animal you wanted to be, which one would you pick? Why? Which animal would you least like to be? Why?

4. What can horses do that people can't?

5. What can horses be used for?

ACTIVITIES
1. Study different kinds of horses – pinto, palomino, quarter horse, etc.

2. Invite a rancher, jockey, horse trainer, or someone else who works with horses to speak to the class.

3. Draw pictures showing the transformation of a person into a horse.

OX-CART MAN

written by Donald Hall
illustrated by Barbara Cooney
published by Viking, 1979

ABOUT THE BOOK

A nineteenth century New England farmer travels to market to sell the items his family grows or makes all year. He buys new supplies and returns home.

FOR DISCUSSION

1. How long do you think the man's trip took?

2. Why do you think the rest of the family stayed home?

3. Why do you think the man sold the ox, cart, harness, etc.?

4. Would you like to have lived in those days? Why or why not?

5. How has travel changed since those days? How is it alike? How has making a living changed? How is it alike?

ACTIVITIES

1. Designate a country store and a modern store. List items and possible prices of items to be found in each. Compare the items. How are they alike and different?

2. Sample wintergreen candy and other "old-fashioned" items.

3. Make a "patchwork quilt" out of a bulletin board. Design a square. Then, together with your classmates, attach the squares together to the bulletin board.

1981

FABLES

written and illustrated by Arnold Lobel
published by Harper, 1980

ABOUT THE BOOK

Twenty fables in contemporary settings are complete with a witty maxim. A variety of animals teach lessons in the fables similar to Aesop's.

FOR DISCUSSION

1. Which fable is your favorite and which is your least favorite? Why?

2. Why do you think the author chose the particular animals he did for each fable?

3. What other books do you know that have a moral or lesson?

4. Do the animals in the fables remind you of any people you know? Why or why not?

5. In which fable do you most recognize yourself?

ACTIVITIES

1. Read Aesop's fables and compare those with Lobel's.

2. Make up your own fable. Duplicate everyone's story to make "books."

3. Draw or paint a picture that shows the moral from one of the fables.

JUMANJI

written and illustrated by Chris Van Allsburg
published by Houghton Mifflin, 1981

ABOUT THE BOOK

A brother and sister play a board game they find in the park. Each move results in a live-action jungle scene in their house.

FOR DISCUSSION

1. Would you like to play Jumanji? Why or why not?

2. What other things could have happened while playing the game?

3. What would you do to save yourself from a lion? A python? Sleeping sickness? An erupting volcano? A monsoon? Being lost? A rhinoceros? Monkeys? A flood?

4. What do you think happened when Danny and Walter played the game without reading the instructions?

5. The illustrator is also a sculptor. What evidence in the illustrations hints of his sculpting talent? Would the illustrations be more effective in color? Why or why not?

ACTIVITIES

1. Find or draw pictures of the pitfalls to cut out to make a collage, or make a sculpture of them from clay.

2. Make a bulletin board of the Jumanji board or a similar game board. Use photos of the students as markers.

3. Make up a game similar to Jumanji. Pick a theme such as your school (pitfalls could include being sent to the principal's office, etc.) or your city (pitfalls could include the jail, etc.). Make a board with squares for pitfalls ("lose one turn for sleeping in school," etc.) and advances ("advance two spaces for a perfect paper," etc.) for the game. Use spinners, dice, or cards to advance spaces.

1983

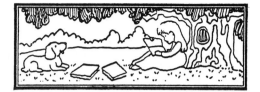

SHADOW

translated and illustrated by Marcia Brown
published by Scribner, 1982

ABOUT THE BOOK
The "Shadow" from African traditions is described as mute, blind, magic, a dance, and a game among other things.

FOR DISCUSSION
1. What do you think Shadow is? Why?

2. What other ways could you describe Shadow?

3. *Shadow* is set in Africa. How would the book be different if it were set in your area?

4. What causes shadows? (The sun, lamps, etc.)

5. Why are shadows sometimes tall and sometimes short?

ACTIVITIES
1. Place an object with an interesting shape on sun-sensitive paper in the sunlight. Develop in tap water. An alternative method is to place the object on dark construction paper and let it sit in the sunlight a few days.

2. Have a fellow classmate make a silhouette of your profile. He or she should shine a flashlight or other light to create a shadow, and lightly pencil the outline on a piece of paper. Write information about yourself (name, age, favorite food, etc.) inside the silhouette. This makes an attractive Mother's Day or Father's Day gift.

3. Make a shadow clock. Punch a pencil through the center of a paper plate. Mark and label the place where the pencil's shadow falls each hour on the hour during the day. The next day you will have a sundial.

THE GLORIOUS FLIGHT: ACROSS THE CHANNEL WITH LOUIS BLERIOT JULY 25, 1919

written and illustrated by Alice and Martin Provensen
published by Viking, 1983

ABOUT THE BOOK

Louis Bleriot goes for a drive with his family and sees a great white airship. He is inspired to build his own flying machine. Finally, on July 25, 1909, he makes a historic solo flight across the English Channel.

FOR DISCUSSION

1. Would you keep trying after the first planes failed? Why or why not?

2. How do you think Louis' family felt as he flew across the channel?

3. How has flight changed since the time Louis flew?

4. Would you like to pilot a plane? Why or why not?

5. For those who have flown, what were your thoughts and feelings at takeoff? In the air? Landing?

ACTIVITIES

1. Find Cambrai, France, and the English Channel on a map.

2. Find other information on Louis Bleriot and/or the Wright Brothers.

3. Conduct a paper airplane contest. Select winners in categories such as the prettiest, one that flies the farthest, one that flies the highest, etc.

1985

SAINT GEORGE AND THE DRAGON

retold by Margaret Hodges
illustrated by Trina Schart Hyman
published by Little Brown, 1984

ABOUT THE BOOK

The Red Cross Knight battles a dragon again and again until he finally
defeats it. He marries a princess and eventually becomes known as
"St. George."

FOR DISCUSSION

1. What are good and bad things about dragons?

2. How would you battle a dragon?

3. How would this story be different if the dragon told it?

4. What do you think a dragon's skin feels like?

5. Why do you think a dragon is a mascot for school teams?

ACTIVITIES

1. Make a three-dimensional dragon out of clay or folded construction paper.

2. Research dragons and/or St. George.

3. Put on a pretend battle that follows the movements described in the books.

THE POLAR EXPRESS

written and illustrated by Chris Van Allsburg
published by Houghton Mifflin, 1985

ABOUT THE BOOK

Late one Christmas Eve, a boy travels by train to the North Pole. Santa gives him a bell, but the boy loses it on the way home. He finds the bell under the tree in the morning.

FOR DISCUSSION

1. Would you like to go to the North Pole? Why or why not? How long do you think the trip would take? Why?

2. How do you think the boy felt at various times throughout the book?

3. How would the story be different if the family opened their gifts on Christmas Eve instead of Christmas morning?

4. If Santa asked you to select a gift, what would you choose? Why?

5. Do you have a possession that you think is special and others don't understand why? Why is it special to you and not to others?

ACTIVITIES

1. Compare the sounds of different kinds of bells.

2. Trace a possible route by air and by land to the North Pole from your location.

3. Ask your teacher to set up an electric train set. Take turns being the engineer.

HEY, AL

written by Arthur Yorinks
illustrated by Richard Egielski
published by Farrar, 1986

ABOUT THE BOOK

A janitor and his dog escape to an island in the sky. One morning they awake to find themselves turning into birds. After a thrilling escape, they discover home can be wonderful, too.

FOR DISCUSSION

1. Do you think Al and Eddie liked each other? Why or why not?

2. Why do you think Al was unhappy being a janitor and living in his apartment in New York?

3. What could Al do to make his life in New York better?

4. Would you like to be a bird? Why or why not? If yes, what kind of bird? Why?

5. What would your idea of paradise be like?

ACTIVITIES

1. Draw or paint a picture of Al and Eddie transforming into other animals besides birds.

2. Select a bird to research. Make sure it is different than those already chosen.

3. Make a list of the good and bad things about your home. What can you do to make the bad things better?

OWL MOON

written by Jane Yolen
illustrated by John Schoenherr
published by Philomel, 1987

ABOUT THE BOOK

A father and child go for a walk during a silent winter night. The father calls "Whoo-who-who-who-whooooooo" to the owls until an owl answers.

FOR DISCUSSION

1. Why do you think the experience of owling was special for the child? The father?

2. If they hadn't found the owl, do you think they still would have enjoyed themselves? Why or why not?

3. What would be the good and bad things about going owling?

4. Would you like to go owling? Why or why not? Who would you like to go with? Why?

5. What could be a similar story about another bird or animal?

ACTIVITIES

1. Go owling or search for another bird or animal. Tell or write about the experience.

2. Listen to a recording of owls and/or other bird sounds.

3. Make a pinecone owl. Use a pinecone for the body. Cut feet, beak, and large round eyes out of felt or construction paper; then glue them to the pinecone.

SONG AND DANCE MAN

written by Karen Ackerman
illustrated by Stephen Gammell
published by Knopf, 1988

ABOUT THE BOOK
Grandpa, a former vaudeville performer, takes his grandchildren to the attic. Grandpa puts on an act using his bowler hat, tap shoes, and a cane.

FOR DISCUSSION
1. Would you like a grandpa like the one in this book? Why or why not?

2. Do you think Grandpa enjoyed performing vaudeville? Why or why not? In the attic? Why or why not?

3. Would you have enjoyed living during the time vaudeville was popular? Why or why not?

4. Would you enjoy a vaudeville show? Why or why not? What types of acts besides those mentioned in the book are there?

5. What do or did your grandparents do for a living?

ACTIVITIES
1. Invite a senior citizen to talk about life during vaudeville days.

2. Put on your own vaudeville show. Do magic tricks, sing, dance, tell jokes, etc.

3. Watch a film of an "old-time" variety show.

LON PO PO: A RED-RIDING HOOD STORY FROM CHINA

retold and illustrated by Ed Young
published by Philomel, 1989

ABOUT THE BOOK

In this version of Red-Riding Hood, Mother goes to visit Grandmother (Po Po) and the wolf comes to the children's home. The children devise a unique way to outwit the wolf.

FOR DISCUSSION

1. Why do you think the book is subtitled *A Red-Riding Hood Story from China*?

2. What are the similarities to the familiar *Red-Riding Hood* story? Differences?

3. Do you like this book better, not as well, or the same as the familiar story? Why?

4. How else could the children have escaped the wolf?

5. In this story the grandmother is called "Po Po." What are other names for "grandmother"? (Examples: Grandma, Gram, Granny, etc.)

ACTIVITIES

1. Sample several kinds of nuts (cashews, peanuts, walnuts, almonds, etc.). Take a survey of the favorites.

2. Make a replica of the wolf in the basket and hang from the ceiling or from the Christmas tree.

3. Paint or draw Chinese panels such as those in the story. Use three or four separate sheets of paper and paint or draw related scenes.

1991

BLACK AND WHITE

written and illustrated by David Macaulay
published by Houghton Mifflin, 1990

ABOUT THE BOOK
The four stories—"Seeing Things, " "Problem Parents," "A Waiting Game,"
and "Udder Chaos"—can be read separately, or interwoven to make one story,
depending upon how you approach them.

FOR DISCUSSION
1. Why do you think the author called this book *Black and White?*

2. Which "story" do you like best? Why? Least? Why?

3. When and where do you sometimes have to wait? What can you do to help
time pass more quickly while you wait?

4. What have your parents done that you think is silly?

5. Which story's illustrations do you like the best? Why? Least? Why?

ACTIVITIES
1. Cut words out of a newspaper or magazine and rearrange them to make
new sentences or even a whole new story.

2. Study the different types of cows—Holstein, Hereford, Angus, etc.

3. Find a book on Origami or other paper-folding techniques and practice
making objects out of newspaper or other paper.

TUESDAY

illustrated and conceived by David Wiesner
published by Clarion, 1991

ABOUT THE BOOK

In this virtually wordless book, frogs on their lilypads rise up and float through the air on a "TUESDAY EVENING, AROUND EIGHT." They have many adventures before they return to earth. Pigs start floating through the air on the "NEXT TUESDAY, 7:58 P.M."

FOR DISCUSSION

1. Why do you think the frogs and pigs were able to fly? Why do you think it was a Tuesday instead of another day of the week?

2. What do you think the people and animals thought when they saw the frogs flying?

3. The frogs ran into some laundry hanging on a line and were chased by dogs. What other hazards do you think they may have encountered?

4. How do you think the police officers explained the lilypads on the street?

5. Would you like to see frogs or pigs fly? Why or why not? Would you like to fly yourself? Why or why not?

ACTIVITIES

1. Play leapfrog.

2. Hang construction paper frogs from the ceiling so that they "fly" in air currents.

3. Research frogs and toads and find out the differences between them. Point out the frogs and the toads in the book.

MIRETTE ON THE HIGH WIRE

written and illustrated by Emily Arnold McCully
published by Putnam, 1992

ABOUT THE BOOK

The Great Bellini, a famous wire-walker, is staying at Mirette's mother's boarding house. Mirette begs him to teach her to wire-walk. She, in turn, helps him overcome his newly-developed fear of the high wire.

FOR DISCUSSION

1. Do you think Mirette's long skirts helped, hurt, or didn't have any affect on her ability to walk on the high wire? Why?

2. Why do you think Mirette kept trying to wire-walk even after she fell several times?

3. Why do you think Bellini became afraid of the high wire?

4. Do you think Mirette's mother would let her go on a world tour? Why or why not?

5. Do you enjoy watching high-wire acts? Why or why not? Would you like to walk the high wire? Why or why not?

ACTIVITIES

1. Practice walking on a narrow plank raised a few inches off the floor.

2. Put on a class circus. Be sure to include a balancing act.

3. Draw or paint a high-wire walker doing something "extra" in the act the way that Bellini fired a cannon and cooked an omelette.

GRANDFATHER'S JOURNEY

written and illustrated by Allen Say
published by Houghton Mifflin, 1993

ABOUT THE BOOK

As a young man, Allen Say's grandfather came to America and traveled across the country. He returned to Japan to marry, but he and his wife moved back to the United States. When their daughter was grown, they moved back to Japan. The grandfather's feelings are torn between the two countries for the remainder of his life.

FOR DISCUSSION

1. Why do you think the grandfather originally left Japan?

2. Why do you think the Pacific Ocean "astonished" the grandfather?

3. Why do you think the grandfather and his wife chose to settle in California instead of Japan or another part of the United States?

4. Why do you think the grandparents returned to Japan only after their daughter was "nearly grown"?

5. What would you miss the most if you moved away from where you currently live?

ACTIVITIES

1. Invite a speaker or speakers who grew up in another country to talk about their childhoods.

2. Find Japan on a map. Figure out the approximate number of miles between Japan and San Francisco and between Japan and where you live.

3. Make a collage of various scenes of life in both urban and rural America. Use pictures of both natural and artificial scenes.

NOTES & UPDATES

NEWBERY BIBLIOGRAPHY
(Alphabetical order by title.) Underlined names indicate illustrator.

Adam Of The Road, Gray, <u>Lawson</u>, Viking, 1942.

Amos Fortune, Free Man, Yates, <u>Unwin</u>, Aladdin, 1950.

Bridge To Terabithia, Paterson, <u>Diamond</u>, Crowell, 1977.

The Bronze Bow, Speare, Houghton Mifflin, 1961.

Caddie Woodlawn, Brink, <u>Seredy, Hyman</u>, Macmillan, 1935.

Call it Courage, <u>Sperry</u>, Macmillan, 1940.

Carry On Mr. Bowditch, Latham, <u>Cosgrave</u>, Houghton Mifflin, 1955.

The Cat Who Went To Heaven, Coatsworth, <u>Ward</u>, Macmillan, 1930.

Daniel Boone, <u>Daugherty</u>, Viking, 1939.

The Dark Frigate, Hawes, <u>Fischer</u>, Little Brown, 1923.

Dear Mr. Henshaw, Cleary, <u>Zelinsky</u>, Morrow, 1983.

Dicey's Song, Voigt, Atheneum, 1982.

Dobry, Shannon, <u>Katchamakoff</u>, Viking, 1934.

The Door In The Wall, <u>Angeli</u>, Viking, 1949.

Mrs. Frisby And The Rats Of Nimh, O'Brien, <u>Bernstein</u>, Atheneum, 1971.

From The Mixed-Up Files Of Mrs. Basil E. Frankweiler, <u>Konigsburg</u>, Atheneum, 1967.

A Gathering Of Days: A New England Girl's Journal 1830-32, Blos, Scribner, 1979.

Gay-Neck, The Story Of A Pigeon, Mukerji, <u>Artzybasheff</u>, Dutton, 1927.

Ginger Pye, <u>Estes</u>, Harcourt, 1951.

The Giver, Lowry, Houghton Mifflin, 1993.

The Grey King, Cooper, <u>Heslop</u>, Atheneum, 1975.

The Hero And The Crown, McKinley, Greenwillow, 1984.

M.C. Higgins The Great, Hamilton, Macmillan, 1974.

The High King, Alexander, Holt, 1968.

Hitty: Her First Hundred Years, Field, <u>Lathrop</u>, Macmillan, 1929.

I, Juan De Pareja, Trevino, Farrar, 1965.

Invincible Louisa, Meigs, Little Brown, 1933.

Island Of The Blue Dolphins, O'Dell, Houghton Mifflin, 1960.

It's Like This, Cat, Neville, <u>Weiss</u>, Harper, 1963.

Jacob Have I Loved, Paterson, Crowell, 1980.

Johnny Tremain, Forbes, <u>Ward</u>, Houghton Mifflin, 1943.

Joyful Noise: Poems For Two Voices, Fleischman, <u>Beddows</u>, Harper, 1988.

Julie Of The Wolves, George, <u>Schoenherr</u>, Harper, 1972.

King Of The Wind, Henry, <u>Dennis</u>, Rand McNally, 1948.

Lincoln: A Photobiography, Freedman, Clarion, 1987.

Lincoln: A Photobiography, Freedman, Clarion, 1987.

The Matchlock Gun, Edmonds, <u>Lantz</u>, Dodd Mead, 1941.

Miracles On Maple Hill, Sorensen, <u>Krush, Beth and Joe</u>, Harcourt, 1956.

Miss Hickory, Bailey, <u>Gannett</u>, Viking, 1946.

. . . And Now Miguel, Krumgold, <u>Charlot</u>, Crowell, 1953.

Missing May, Rylant, Orchard/Richard Jackson, 1992.

Number The Stars, Lowry, Houghton Mifflin, 1989.

Onion John, Krumgold, <u>Shimin</u>, Crowell, 1959.

Rabbit Hill, <u>Lawson</u>, Viking, 1944.

Rifles For Watie, Keith, Crowell, 1957.

Roll Of Thunder, Hear My Cry, Taylor, Dial, 1976.

Roller Skates, Sawyer, <u>Angelo</u>, Viking, 1936.

Sarah Plain And Tall, MacLachlan, Harper, 1985.

Secret Of The Andes, Clark, <u>Charlot</u>, Viking, 1952.

Shadow Of A Bull, Wojciechowska, <u>Smith</u>, Atheneum, 1964.

Shen Of The Sea, Chrisman, <u>Hasselriis</u>, Dutton, 1925.

Shiloh, Naylor, Atheneum, 1991.

The Slave Dancer, Fox, <u>Keith</u>, Bradbury, 1973.

Smoky, The Cowhorse, James, Scribner, 1926.

Sounder, Armstrong, <u>Barkley</u>, Harper, 1969.

The Story Of Mankind, <u>Loon</u>, Liveright, 1921.

Strawberry Girl, <u>Lenski</u>, Viking, 1945.

Summer Of The Swans, Byars, <u>CoConis</u>, Viking, 1970.

Tales From Silver Lands, Finger, <u>Honore</u>, Doubleday, 1924.

Thimble Summer, <u>Enright</u>, Rinehart, 1938.

The Trumpeter Of Krakow, Kelly, <u>Prusynska, Domanska</u>, Macmillan, 1928

The Twenty-One Balloons, <u>du Bois</u>, Viking, 1947.

Up A Road Slowly, Hunt, Follett, 1966.

A Visit To William Blake's Inn, Willard, <u>Provensen, Alice and Martin</u>, Harcourt, 1981.

The Voyages Of Doctor Dolittle, <u>Lofting</u>, Lippincott, 1922.

Waterless Mountain, Armer, <u>Armer, Sidney and Laura</u>, Longmans, 1931.

The Westing Game, <u>Raskin</u>, Dutton, 1978.

The Wheel On The School, DeJong, <u>Sendak</u>, Harper, 1954.

The Whipping Boy, Fleischman, <u>Sis</u>, Greenwillow, 1986.

The White Stag, <u>Seredy</u>, Viking, 1937.

The Witch Of Blackbird Pond, Speare, Houghton Mifflin, 1958.

A Wrinkle In Time, L'Engle, Farrar, 1962.

Young Fu Of The Upper Yangtze, Lewis, <u>Wiese</u>, Winston, 1932.

CALDECOTT BIBLIOGRAPHY
(Alphabetical order by title.) Underlined names indicate illustrator.

Abraham Lincoln, <u>d' Aulaire, Ingri and Edgar</u>, Doubleday, 1939.

Always Room For One More, adapted by Leodhas, <u>Hogrogian</u>, Holt, 1965.

Animals Of The Bible, Fish, <u>Lathrop</u>, Lippincott, 1937.

Arrow To The Sun, retold by <u>McDermott</u>, Viking, 1974.

Ashanti to Zulu: African Traditions, Musgrove, <u>Dillon, Leo and Diane</u>, Dial, 1976.

Baboushka And The Three Kings, Robbins, <u>Sidjakov</u>, Parnassus Press, 1960.

The Big Snow, <u>Hader, Berta and Elmer</u>, Macmillan, 1948.

The Biggest Bear, <u>Ward</u>, Houghton Mifflin, 1952.

Black and White, <u>Macaulay</u>, Houghton Mifflin, 1990.

Chanticleer And The Fox, <u>Cooney</u>, Viking, 1958.

Cinderella, Or The Little Glass Slipper, <u>Brown</u>, Scribner, 1954.

Drummer Hoff, adapted by Emberley, Barbara, <u>Emberley, Ed</u>, Prentice-Hall, 1967.

Duffy And The Devil, retold by Zemach, Harve, <u>Zemach, Margot</u>, Farrar, 1973.

The Egg Tree, <u>Milhous</u>, Scribner, 1950.

Fables, <u>Lobel</u>, Harper, 1980.

Finders Keepers, Lipkind, <u>Mordvinoff</u>, Harcourt, 1951.

The Fool Of The World And The Flying Ship, retold by Ransome, <u>Shulevitz</u>, Farrar, 1968.

Frog Went A-Courtin', retold by Langstaff, <u>Rojankovsky</u>, Harcourt, 1955.

The Funny Little Woman, retold by Mosel, <u>Lent</u>, Dutton, 1972.

The Girl Who Loved Wild Horses, <u>Gobel</u>, Bradbury, 1978.

The Glorious Flight: Across The Channel With Louis Bleriot July 25, 1919, <u>Provensen, Alice and Martin</u>, Viking, 1983.

Grandfather's Journey, <u>Say</u>, Houghton Mifflin, 1993.

Hey, Al, Yorinks, <u>Egielski</u>, Farrar, 1986.

Jumanji, <u>Van Allsburg</u>, Houghton Mifflin, 1981.

The Little House, <u>Burton</u>, Houghton Mifflin, 1942.

The Little Island, MacDonald, <u>Weisgard</u>, Doubleday, 1946.

Lon Po Po: A Red-Riding Hood Story From China, retold by <u>Young</u>, Philomel, 1989.

Madeline's Rescue, <u>Bemelmans</u>, Viking, 1953.

Make Way For Ducklings, McCloskey, Viking, 1941.

Many Moons, Thurber, Slobodkin, Harcourt, 1943.

May I Bring A Friend? de Regniers, Montresor, Atheneum, 1964.

Mei Li, Handforth, Doubleday, 1938.

Mirette On The High Wire, McCully, Putnam, 1992.

Nine Days To Christmas, Ets and Labastida, Viking, 1959.

Noah's Ark, Spier, Doubleday, 1977.

Once A Mouse, retold by Brown, Scribner, 1961.

One Fine Day, adapted by Hogrogian, Macmillan, 1971.

Owl Moon, Yolen, Schoenherr, Philomel, 1987.

Ox-Cart Man, Hall, Cooney, Viking, 1979.

The Polar Express, Van Allsburg, Houghton Mifflin, 1985.

Prayer For A Child, Field, Jones, Macmillan, 1944.

The Rooster Crows, selected by Petersham, Maud and Miska, Macmillan, 1945.

Saint George And The Dragon, retold by Hodges, Hyman, Little Brown, 1984.

Sam, Bangs And Moonshine, Ness, Holt, 1966.

Shadow, translated by Brown, Scribner, 1982.

The Snowy Day, Keats, Viking, 1962.

Song And Dance Man, Ackerman, Gammell, Knopf, 1988.

Song Of The Swallows, Politi, Scribner, 1949.

A Story, A Story, retold by Haley, Atheneum, 1970.

Sylvester And The Magic Pebble, Steig, Windmill Books, 1969.

They Were Strong And Good, Lawson, Viking, 1940.

Time Of Wonder, McCloskey, Viking, 1957.

A Tree Is Nice, Udry, Simont, Harper, 1956.

Tuesday, Wiesner, Clarion, 1991.

Where The Wild Things Are, Sendak, Harper, 1963.

White Snow, Bright Snow, Tresselt, Duvoisin, Lothrop, 1947.

Why Mosquitoes Buzz In People's Ears, retold by Aardema, Dillon, Leo and Diane, Dial, 1975.